TRANSLATIONS BY ALICE SEDGWICK WOHL

*On Antique Painting*, by Francisco de Hollanda

*The Lives of the Modern Painters, Sculptors and Architects*, by Giovan Pietro Bellori

*The Life of Michelangelo*, by Ascanio Condivi

# As It Turns Out

# As It Turns Out

THINKING ABOUT EDIE AND ANDY

## Alice Sedgwick Wohl

FARRAR, STRAUS AND GIROUX ▪ NEW YORK

Farrar, Straus and Giroux
120 Broadway, New York 10271

Owing to limitations of space, all acknowledgments for permission to
reprint previously published material can be found on page 257.

Illustration credits can be found on page 259.

Library of Congress Cataloging-in-Publication Data
Names: Wohl, Alice Sedgwick, author.
Title: As it turns out : thinking about Edie and Andy / Alice Sedgwick Wohl.
Description: First edition. | New York : Farrar, Straus and Giroux, 2022. |
    Includes bibliographical references.
Identifiers: LCCN 2022018293 | ISBN 9780374604684 (hardcover)
Subjects: LCSH: Sedgwick, Edie. | Wohl, Alice Sedgwick—Family. |
    Warhol, Andy, 1928–1987—Friends and associates. | Motion picture
    actors and actresses—United States—Biography. | Models (Persons)—
    United States—Biography. | Socialites—United States—Biography.
    Classification: LCC PN2287.S3445 W64 2022 | DDC 791.4302/8092
    [B]—dc23/eng/20220505
LC record available at  https://lccn.loc.gov/2022018293

*Designed by Gretchen Achilles*

# CONTENTS

Spring 2019      3

The Past      9

1965      119

Notes for My Dead Brother      195

Notes      245

Acknowledgments      253

# As It Turns Out

*I have outlived my brother Bobby by more than fifty years now, and ever since he died I have been talking to him and making notes in my mind. I'm told that happens when you lose a sibling to whom you're close: you're left with a phantom presence, like an amputee with a phantom limb. It's not that I keep track of anything systematically, I just find myself stopping from time to time to fix particular perceptions and ideas, trying to imagine what he would think, because things here have been going in a direction that neither he nor I would ever have anticipated. In the sixties, it was clear that a big shift was taking place, and from our different vantage points we were both hopeful, but as it turned out, it was not the radical social and political change that either of us was looking for. Instead, it turned out to be a shift in an entirely new direction, one that had to do with what Andy Warhol and our sister Edie Sedgwick represented when they got together in 1965. But Bobby didn't live to see that, and I wasn't paying attention.*

*And then, a couple of years ago, I happened to be visiting the Addison Gallery at Andover with my husband, and there on the top floor I suddenly came upon two very large images of Edie. Two*

3

close-ups of her head and face side by side on a film screen—one bright, one dark, in velvety blacks and chalky whites against a flat black ground.

I knew it had to be a clip from a Warhol film I'd read about called Outer and Inner Space, because what I was seeing was the image of a "real" Edie at the right responding to a video image of herself on a television monitor at the left and relaying her reactions to someone outside the frame. The monitor screen is large, and Edie's face occupies it completely. She appears in profile, with her head tilted upward and fully illuminated so that her skin is pure white and her silvered hair shines. She looks up steadily with wide-open eyes and an inquiring, almost visionary, expression, while her lips seem to be forming words in slow motion, although I don't remember any sound. The "real" Edie's face is darker, and it's also smaller, so at first I didn't understand that this Edie is not behind or even beside the video image; instead, she's in front of it—you can see her shoulder. So she's not actually seeing her image, she's listening to it and responding to what she hears  .  .  .  Her face is partly in shadow and further darkened by the sooty makeup around her eyes, and it's framed by a pair of very long, dangly earrings that cast complex shadows on her neck as she moves. She's never still. She reacts to every least nuance. She's smoking, and a lot of the time she's talking, but again, I don't remember the sound. At first I was startled just to see Edie so alive and vital, when she'd been dead for nearly half a century, but what astonished me was the presence she had on camera. I couldn't take my eyes off her. At the same time, I thought I was seeing a very complex play upon the figure of Narcissus, the beautiful Greek boy who fell fatally in love with his own image. But what I was really seeing, and seeing for the first time, was what Andy Warhol made of Edie Sedgwick.

*I was completely stunned: stunned by Edie, stunned by all the layers and dimensions I was perceiving in the film, and above all stunned to realize what I had missed all these years. I know Bobby recognized something powerful in Edie, and I know he would have understood at the time what Warhol was up to. But in all honesty I don't think I would have, even if I hadn't been so badly shaken by our brother Minty's death and then his.*

*Because this is how I found out. The telephone rang in the middle of the night in the apartment on West Ninetieth Street. I picked up the receiver and it was our father's voice saying, "Minty hanged himself today." Just like that. I had been sound asleep when he called, and I had a six-week-old baby sleeping in the next room. I began to tremble all over. An abyss opened and there it was, the absolute, black finality of death. Twist and turn as I might in the next hours and days, nothing more was possible. It was March 4, 1964; the next day he would have been twenty-seven years old. Then on New Year's Day, some ten months later, I came home and there was an unsigned telegram under the door. (It was a long time before I realized it could only have come from our parents, and it meant they didn't want to have to talk to me.) It said Bobby had had an accident, that he was in Saint Vincent's in intensive care. When I got down there, I found him lying very still with a bandage covering his head. I took his big heavy hand, and from under the bandage tears leaked down his cheeks. Then the doctor came along and said it was the tubes irritating his nose. Some days later, on the phone, that same doctor said they were going to take him off life support. I had not understood, and I wanted to know what would happen. He said, "Well, he'll just poop out." Those were his exact words. So Bobby died too, and because he had crashed his motorcycle into a city bus, I had to go to the New York City morgue to identify him.*

*I was shown into a dark chamber, a light flashed on, and there he was, handsome as ever, lying on a shelf in the wall. I gasped, the light flashed off, and the attendant let me out. Afterward, for a long time, I saw in my mind a bare branch sticking out of a swiftly flowing river. The branch was unmoving, but I was moving away from it, upstream against the current.*

*Edie had come to New York in the summer of '64, and she was already exploding like a firework in the sky. Bobby had seen her in Cambridge in the spring, and it was as if he'd never known her before, he was so taken with her. I'm not sure if he was still an active Communist at that point, but if so he certainly forgot about it when he was with Edie. He was ten years older and so intensely political, and as far as I could see she was just a silly, spoiled child full of problems. When Christmas came round, he wanted her to stay in New York and spend it with him, but Edie listened to our parents and went home to the ranch. Then when she came back he was dead. A couple of months passed, and one night she went to a party given by a producer of commercials called Lester Persky, who thought she might appeal to his friend Andy Warhol.*

*That was the beginning of everything that I'm trying to think about now. I'm trying to figure out exactly what happened when Edie got together with Andy. I want to know what she had that I so totally failed to see, but that he saw and put to such effective use. I want to understand what he was up to, because right now it seems to me that when the two of them got together something was set in motion that led to the present that we are all living out. Edie is absolutely part of the present: to my surprise kids in high school know about her, and her image is everywhere. Open a glossy magazine, there's a piece on the American ambassador's residence in Paris, and what's hanging on the wall? The photograph of Andy in the* manhole holding a camera and Edie behind him with her legs in the air. Go into a bookstore and there's a new book about Warhol full of pictures of Edie, and, of course, if you look her up on the internet, there's no end to what you can find, and all of it seems as if it just happened.

Some kind of disjunction must have taken place, because when I call up images of the life we lived as a family and the rich disintegrating fabric of the past that formed us, it all seems very, very remote . . .

# THE PAST

Alice de Forest and Francis Minturn (Duke) Sedgwick
on their wedding day, May 9, 1929

# I

When they were young, in the 1930s, our parents divided the year between California and Long Island. They spent the summer months in Goleta, in the foothills west of Santa Barbara, at a place that had been a wedding present from our mother's parents. They hadn't wanted her to marry my father: she was nineteen and he was twenty-three when he proposed, and although he was very handsome and came of an old New England family, he had a history of nervous trouble. But she was determined, and eventually they gave in. The marriage took place in New York, at Grace Church, on May 9, 1929, and oh, how radiant they were as they stepped out of the church, the former Alice de Forest and her new husband, Francis Minturn Sedgwick, he in his cutaway and she in a satin dress with a veil of tulle and old lace, carrying her train and a big beribboned bouquet. They spent their honeymoon in California, at the place in Goleta, which even now, more than eighty years later, I remember as paradise.

The house stood—indeed may still stand—facing south in a vast sweep of landscape that descended from the Sierra Madre to the coast. In style it was Spanish: one storey, white stucco with a tiled roof, and built around a patio. Plumbago and trumpet-flower vines and scarlet bougainvillea covered the outer walls so you could hardly find the yellow front door, and the patio was filled with flowering shrubs that sent their fragrance floating in through the windows. Outside the living room there was a large covered terrace lined with ivy, and an open terrace above it where our parents sometimes slept on clear nights. That side of the house looked out over steep gardens and orchards of orange and lemon trees and beyond, across open countryside studded with stands of eucalyptus to the ocean and the Channel Islands. Behind the house there was a cavernous white barn that served as the garage, and built onto the back of it was our father's studio, where they gave parties that we could hear from our beds in the house. From there the land rose to a tawny hilltop where our parents had built a tennis court and a pool, each in its green wire cage, as well as another cage enclosing a sandbox and swings. Farther on, almost out of sight, there was a rough riding ring with jumps and a little wooden cabin lined with blue ribbons our mother had won before she married. Now our parents always rode together. If we children were in the playground, we could see them go by in the distance and disappear toward the foothills that rolled, yellow and sage blue, all the way up to the mountains. The sky above was immense, full of buzzards wheeling high up, and once the morning fog burned off it was blue, always blue, because in that place it was always summer.

Bobby and I were born there, I in the summer of 1931 and he two years later; however, our mother was not to have another child in California until Edie came along, and meanwhile our sister Pamela and the next three—Minty and Jonathan and Kate—were all born in a different climate and another landscape altogether.

Until the war, we spent the rest of the year on Long Island, first at our mother's family place in Cold Spring Harbor, where we stayed until Pamela was born, and eventually in a

*(top)* Painting by Duke Sedgwick of the house in Goleta, 1930s

*(bottom)* Painting by Duke Sedgwick of the view from the house, 1930s

large white clapboard house of our own on a pond a couple of miles away. There we three older children lived with Sophie, our dour gray-haired German governess, on the third floor, in little irregular rooms under the eaves. The doors all opened onto a large playroom that contained a big wooden table for Bobby's Lionel trains, some chests stuffed with toys and tools and games, and a golden-brown hobby horse with real hide and hair. All around, the walls were lined with low shelves full of books. I remember distinctly the different worlds evoked by the illustrations of Kate Greenaway and Arthur Rackham and Howard Pyle, but what I liked best was a set of *St. Nicholas Magazine* from the years 1910–1920 bound in large red leather volumes embossed in gold. I remember poring over the pictures—soldiers in jodhpurs and women in white uniforms standing beside ambulances, people in wooden boats hurtling across a frozen river, old ladies in long black dresses sitting on porches—trying to imagine what life might hold for me. There was a skylight over the playroom, but otherwise the house was dark, and in my memory the landscape outside was mostly dark as well. Blacks and browns and dull silver were the colors of the pond and the woods that rose from its margins, although in spring a queer pale green broke out on the trees, and the dogwoods bloomed.

The house stood on a wide sloping lawn between the pond and the road, which was out of sight behind a high gray cinder-block wall. Our parents built that wall to keep out the noise of passing cars, and even as a small child I was ashamed of it. I read English children's books and I knew that walls were supposed to be made of brick or stone, and houses too, for that matter. The other thing I was ashamed of was our car, not the cars our parents drove but the one in which we were taken to the school bus. It was a pinkish-beige delivery van like the Dugan bread truck, fitted with pearl-gray vinyl seats. The other children came in station wagons with wooden sides, except for the Coes, who were driven all the way to school in a limousine.

The main thing I remember about that house in Cold Spring Harbor is all the rules. In our family the basic methods of child-rearing were disciplinary: rules, admonitions, criticism, shaming, and spanking were the degrees, and the rules concerned not only our behavior but also our manners and speech. Do as you are told. Don't talk back. Ask "May I?," not "Can I?" Don't brag, don't show off, don't draw attention to yourself. Curtsy when you are introduced to a grown-up, look them in the eye and say, "How do you do," never say "Hello." Never address adults by their first names unless, of course, you are speaking to a servant.

The rules for table manners were endless: rest your left hand on the table, just the hand, not the forearm, never the elbow; hold the soup spoon parallel to your lips and dip it away from you; do *not* switch your knife and fork after cutting your meat. We learned to eat what was on our plates, because if we didn't the plates would reappear at every meal until we did. Bobby and I dropped unwanted food behind the radiator, but Pamela put so many peas up her nose she had to be taken to the doctor.

There were rules for other eventualities as well. I learned that in public I should never let myself be seen entering or leaving a bathroom, and that I should always run the water so nothing I did could be heard. I also learned that it was wrong

15

to begin a letter or even a paragraph with the pronoun "I," and that I should always sign my name in my regular handwriting. No fancy signatures. Mainly, we learned to do as we were told and not to ask questions, particularly not where we were going or what was going to happen. "Wait and see" was the invariable response, even years later on the ranch, when we wanted to know where we were going to ride or whether we were going to town.

Then there were rules about language: we say "house," "letter-paper," and "trousers," never "home," "stationery," or "pants." All the children we knew called their mothers "Mummy"; no one said "Mommy" or "Mom." They called their fathers "Daddy" or sometimes "Pop," but we called ours "Fuzzy," which was understood to be special, meaning something about him. Along with usage, we were taught pronunciation: not to talk through our noses, never to pronounce final Rs, and to say some words in a particular way. So when we moved to California for good, the other children in school would amuse themselves by asking me to say words like "orange," "garage," and particularly "squirrel," which they pronounced "awrnge," "grodge," and "squirl." And when I got to college a girl asked in front of a lot of people where I got my accent. I said I got it from my parents. She said her parents had a Yiddish accent, she had had to make up her own, and what did I think of that?

The house in Cold Spring Harbor had many levels, and so did the household. At the top was our father, who was the most inaccessible, in part because his interests didn't include us and in part because he was gone all day. He would be driven to the station like everybody else's father, wearing a dark suit and a coat and hat, but unlike them he didn't go to an office. He went to his studio because he was an artist. Our mother was at home, but unless we got into trouble we mainly saw her at meals, except for supper, which we had at five-thirty. We could hear her during the day practicing the piano or talking on the telephone. After her mastoid operation went wrong, however, she began taking me with her when she went out to do errands or to see Dr. Wallig in Sea Cliff for electric treatments on her face. One side was smooth and drooping, so she only had half a smile, and from time to time her eyes rolled, especially the one on the droopy side. But nothing was ever said, and I am shocked now to realize how matter-of-factly we children accepted the change. The thing is, our mother's self-control was such that there was absolutely no difference in her behavior. She was in her late twenties then, and she had been quite beautiful, a bit like Edie but more ladylike, and our father was so very handsome, so proud of his thick hair and fine physique.

We did see her if we got into trouble. Sophie was strict, and she could deal with manners and habits and ordinary misbehavior, but any real naughtiness was reported to our mother, who would lecture us and mete out minor punishments. In the case of egregious misdeeds and faults of character, however, she would shake her head and say that she had no choice but to tell our father when he came home. That meant hours of terror and abject behavior, because he never sent for us right away but waited until after our supper, after he had exercised and bathed and dressed for dinner, before spanking us. Three or four sharp smacks of a hairbrush on our bare bottoms, then he would comfort us and say it hurt him more than it did us.

I say "us," but it was usually me, because Bobby was diffident and kept to himself and Pamela was a very cautious and obedient child. I, on the other hand, was overeager and heedless, and to make matters worse, the instant I found myself in trouble I would try to lie my way out of it. It was not until late adolescence that I understood that the truth as I knew it to be was the only thing in the world I could count on.

Next in the hierarchy, but well below our parents, came Sophie, with whom we lived and had our meals. There was also a series of nurses called Nana for the younger children, but they stayed upstairs in the nursery, especially if there was a new baby. Then came the Scottish butler, William Kennedy, and his French wife, who was the cook. Her real name was Jeanne, but she was called Nancy because a previous employer had had another Jean on the staff. We didn't really know Nancy then, because we weren't allowed in the kitchen, but William served in the dining room and drove us to the school bus, so we knew him well. We also knew the Swedish housemaid, a frail and gentle old woman named Karen, who wore a pale green uniform with a white apron and had Thursdays off. We children were at the bottom, no question, and the reason I think Karen was on the same level is that she confided in me: she told me once that she earned sixty dollars a month. Nobody else told me much of anything except what I should and shouldn't do.

There was one person who did talk to me, and that was our grandmother de Forest. We had known her always because when Bobby and I were small our family lived at Nethermuir, the de Forest family place, in an old farmhouse that stood across the lawn but out of sight from the big white house where our grandparents lived. I still have vivid memories of that time, two in particular: I remember being lifted out of my crib by my nanny and carried to the window to see a rainbow, and I remember I had an obsessive mistrust of adults; I thought I had to keep my eyes open all the time I was around them. But the place was beautiful. Both houses overlooked an inlet from Long Island Sound called Cold Spring Harbor, and while the farmhouse was modest, Nethermuir itself was three storeys high, with two lower wings, and terraces and gardens all around. After Grandpa died, which happened when I was seven, Grandma had to sell the place, and she had the big house torn down. She left everything else—the walled garden, the farmhouse, the brown shingled boathouse and its dock, and the huge barn where I was taken to visit a very old man named Lynch who had been the coachman in the days before automobiles. The place had belonged to de Forests for generations, and Grandma didn't want anyone else to live in their house. My mother never forgave her. She grieved for her childhood home, but my father said he couldn't understand how an intelligent man like Grandpa had lost so much of his fortune in the stock market.

After the house was demolished, all the land that bordered on Cold Spring Harbor was sold, and my grandmother moved up the hill and across the road to a formal brick house that was built for Mummy's older sister Molly Duer, who went to live in Virginia instead. I came to know that house well, just as I came to know my grandmother, because I was sent to stay with her whenever I was sick, or whenever our parents went away, to protect the other children from contagion of one kind or another, germs or mischief. That was the way our parents looked at it. The way I looked at it, I got to have the experience of being a beloved only child.

My grandmother told me all kinds of stories about my ancestors, going back before the Revolution, and she loved to talk about her school. She had grown up in Saint Paul, Minnesota, where her father, Charles Phelps Noyes, was in business, and instead of having her taught at home like other girls, her parents had sent her away to the Cambridge School for Girls. Her mother's brother Arthur Gilman, who founded the Women's Annex at Harvard, started that school with his wife to provide an education for their daughters, and Grandma spent three happy years there. I believe it is where she met her life-long closest friend, May Tiffany. May-May, as she was always called, was the daughter of the decorative artist and designer Louis Comfort Tiffany, and she invited Grandma to stay at their country place in Laurel Hollow. Nethermuir was just up the road, and one evening Henry de Forest was asked to dinner. So that's how she met Grandpa. He was nearly forty and already a prominent lawyer and philanthropist in New York, and she was twenty. Years later, I asked if anyone had told her anything before she was married. She said no, she had no idea, but she said on their wedding night Grandpa explained, and she smiled at the memory. She always sounded surprised and honored that he had chosen her, and sometimes she laughed about the difference between their fortunes. I already knew that one was not supposed to talk about money or status, but in her dignified way my grandmother managed to convey quite a lot. At home, instead, not much was conveyed. There I had to learn by observing and guessing, and a lot of the time I guessed wrong.

From our rooms on the top floor we older children could not hear what happened in the rest of the house, unless there was a new baby. Then we could hear harsh squalling, hour after hour. Our mother said that was how babies got their exercise. Sometimes we could hear guests arriving, or the roar of a dinner party, but nothing more because we went to bed early. We kissed our parents good night downstairs (we kissed them; they did not kiss us), and Sophie saw us up to bed. Before getting in, we had to kneel and ask God to bless our father and mother and one another and to take our souls if we died in the night. I don't know whose idea that was, because we were not baptized until there got to be three or four of us. Then one spring day our great-uncle the Reverend Theodore Sedgwick, an old gentleman with a beaky nose, came from Connecticut, put on a robe with a billowing white garment over it, and christened us all in a batch on the terrace.

We had been going to church for a while by then, but it was a case of "Do as I say, not as I do," because our parents never went, and once when I told Fuzzy that I was going to be the angel Gabriel in the pageant he laughed out loud. The plain white clapboard church, which the de Forest family had attended forever, stood diagonally across the pond from our house, and we walked there by ourselves. Sophie didn't come because she was Catholic, but sometimes the dogs would follow us and pelt down the aisle, misbehaving until somebody put them out and made sure they stayed.

For as long as I can remember, our parents always had dogs. The ones I remember particularly from Cold Spring Harbor days are Woof, a lolloping creature that was half greyhound and half Great Dane, and Quichee, my father's English bull terrier. Quichee was squat and white, with a muzzle like an alligator, and because he was always getting into fights, he usually had nasty puncture wounds that the vet painted blue. I was terrified of him and those holes in his skin. One time on the train to California he was recovering from a fight, and I was shut up in a compartment alone with him and told to wait there because my mother wanted to talk to me. After a while she came and brought a book with a pale green cloth cover that had birds and flowers incised on it in gold. Quichee was sitting there by the window and she sat down next to him and told me in a very roundabout way how babies were made, which she said was all very wonderful; then she stood up, confided that she was going to have a baby in December (I guess it was Jonathan, because I must have been seven or eight), and went out again, leaving me with the book and the dog. I was flattered and excited, and when Sophie came I burst out with what I had learned. It turned out I was not supposed to talk about any of it, including the baby.

Except for Quichee that once, the dogs did not ride with us in the railway car when we went to California. I don't know how they traveled, but one time they got loose in Grand Central and raced around the tracks. Our mother had all the trains stopped until they could be caught. Perhaps the stationmaster would have done this for anyone, but we always assumed it was because Grandpa had been president of the Southern Pacific for a time and had his own private car, called the Airslie. Our family did not have a railway car, of course, but eventually there were so many of us that we had one to ourselves.

The trip took five days, but it was always broken in Chicago, where we would get off and have breakfast at the Blackstone

Hotel while the car was switched to a different train for the journey west. I have no recollection of leaving Chicago, but I can still see in my mind an endless flat landscape dotted with wooden farm buildings and spindly windmills made of metal, and the continuous loop-loop-loop of telephone wires that stopped when we passed through a town and started up again right away as we left. The train would hoot and rattle through stations and past platforms, and it must have stopped at some of them, but the only place I remember clearly was in the middle of the desert. I don't think there was any station there at all. It was just a sandy place where Indians crowded below our windows, holding up rugs and baskets and jewelry, and I remember one time Sophie bought a turquoise ring. After that the landscape would be dry and jagged for a day or two until we came to California; then there was the unspeakable joy of arriving in Santa Barbara.

I know our parents were happy there too, at least in the early years, because I remember them singing all the time and calling each other "darling." They rode and they swam and they played tennis with their friends, who were in and out all the time, talking and laughing. The sun always shone, the air was always fragrant, and the vegetation seemed to be forever in flower, alive with butterflies and hummingbirds and large noisy bees. Even the food was delicious. We often had lunch out-of-doors, on the terrace or up by the pool, and quite often guests would come for a game of tennis and stay on. After lunch, if there were no guests, our mother would sometimes go calling in Santa Barbara, visiting soft-spoken older people who lived in large quiet houses, and sometimes she took me with her. I remember on the way to Montecito one day we passed a big park where groups of ragged men were sitting and lying about under the trees. I asked Mummy who they were and she said they were called "hobos" and that a lady was being very kind, letting them live in such a beautiful place. After that when a freight train passed I could sometimes see hobos hanging out the open doors, but I don't recall asking any more questions. Nor did I think anything of it when dark-skinned men from Mexico were brought all packed together in the open backs of trucks to pick the fruit in our orchards.

The first I ever heard of politics was in Long Island in 1940, when Roosevelt was running for reelection again and Wendell Wilkie ran against him. Grandma wore a pin with Wilkie's name on it, but I don't remember anyone mentioning the subject at home. I did hear it discussed at school, where almost everybody was wearing buttons like Grandma's and making fun of FDR and Mrs. Roosevelt and their dog Fala. (Grandma actually voted for FDR once, but she said that was only because Grandpa told her any child of Sarah and Jimmy's would make a good governor.) Roosevelt won, and at school I began hearing about war. I had known about the Germans invading France, because that's why Grandma had gone there on a boat, to a place called Pau, and brought her elderly aunt Serena Davenport home to live with her. I was impressed by my great-great-aunt: she was the widow of an admiral who fought in the Spanish-American War, and she wore stiff black dresses down to her feet just like all the old ladies in *St. Nicholas Magazine*. I had also heard that England was at war with Germany, although at home nobody talked about it. Life went on, and the following year, on December 6, my mother had another baby, a girl they named Katherine

Sedgwick family, six children, in Cold Spring Harbor, spring 1942

and wound up calling Kate, although people at the hospital thought she should be called Pearl because the next day the Japanese bombed Pearl Harbor. Then America declared war, and at school we began making patriotic drawings and singing military songs.

At home our parents talked about their friends enlisting and going off to war. Uncle Minturn, Fuzzy's handsome older brother, came to say goodbye because he was joining the air force and going to London. I am not sure how I learned that Fuzzy himself couldn't get into the service, or that he was embarrassed when people looked at him, knowing they saw a healthy young man in civilian clothes. They couldn't know that he had very bad asthma or that he had six children, which was one more reason, so they said. But now I realize there might have been something else: he had had a couple of nervous breakdowns, and that must have been in his records. His psychiatrist sent a letter of recommendation, but he was rejected anyway. I learned that some thirty years later, which is when I also learned that the same psychiatrist had warned my mother and father before they were married that they should not have children.

One dark morning that same winter, we older ones were sitting at the round table in the corner of the dining room having breakfast when Nancy suddenly came in all excited and told us Mummy and Fuzzy had bought a big ranch in California, with pigs and chickens and lots of cows, and we were all going out there to live. Sophie already knew, but no one had said anything to us. Nor did anybody tell us our grandfather Sedgwick, our beloved Babbo, was going to live there with us.

## II

So it was that we found ourselves in the Santa Ynez Valley, over the mountains from Santa Barbara, on a ranch called Corral de Quati. The strange thing, given that everything was so very different from anything I had ever known, is that I have no recollection of arriving; we were simply there, on

Duke and Alice Sedgwick on their new gray mares
at Corral de Quati, 1942

three thousand acres of tawny yellow tableland dotted with
live oaks and brown-and-white Hereford cattle. The ranch
was easy to find. You came off the road from Los Olivos and
up a little rise, and the buildings were all right there, laid out
around a large oval pasture: barns, corrals, and sheds on one
side, the main house opposite, cottages for the men at either
end. The house was low and L-shaped, with yellow walls and
brown shutters and trim and a small flowerless garden with a
picket fence. Outside the gate stood a clump of pepper trees
and a wooden frame with a large bronze bell that was rung

half an hour before meals to call us from the barns or wherever we were, and again when the meal was ready.

The house was dead simple. It was built all on one level, and composed of enclaves. Our parents had their quarters in one corner, off the living room; William and Nancy had theirs in the opposite corner, off the kitchen; Minty and Jonathan and Kate lived with Sophie in the middle of the wing that faced the garden; and our grandfather Babbo lived at the end, where he had a large room next to the spare room. Beyond that was the bathroom, which he had to share with us older children, who lived outside because there were not enough bedrooms to go round. The three of us each had a little bunkhouse of our own, so placed that we could not see or hear one another, or in other words get into mischief. Bobby's was by the back door to the bathroom, mine was over next to the road, and Pamela's was way around outside the kitchen, probably so William and Nancy could hear her if she cried in the night. She was only six, and I seem to remember that she was unhappy, but I absolutely loved my bunkhouse. It measured some eight by ten feet and contained a bed, a bedside table, a dresser, a wooden chair, and a row of hooks to hang my clothes on. It had electricity—a light bulb hung from the ceiling—but no windows; instead, there were screens all round, so anybody could see in. At night, though, I could hear a whole landscape of sounds: coyotes and owls, all sorts of cries and rustlings, and in summer the raucous buzz of the katydids. Nobody could possibly have heard me if I'd called out.

That suited me just fine, and it showed how differently we were going to live now. So did our clothes: we children wore unironed workshirts and overalls or jeans, and brown lace-up shoes that were good for our feet, which our riding boots supposedly were not. On the whole we were pretty disheveled and not particularly clean, and it was clear we belonged to a different class from our parents, who always looked perfect. Fuzzy dressed like a cowboy, hat and all. In summer he wore clean pressed jeans with a wide belt and tight little blue T-shirts that showed off his muscular physique, and when it got cold, he changed to gabardine trousers and soft yellow chamois shirts. And always before getting on his horse, he would buckle on his big leather chaps. In contrast, our mother wore English riding clothes that she had made for her in New York: jodhpurs and low strapped boots and tweed coats or gabardine, according to the season. Although my father looked impressive on a horse, she was the one the cowboys admired. She was a really good rider.

Our clothes were not the only thing that was different: while Sophie kept an eye on the others, Bobby and I were completely unsupervised now except in the immediate presence of our parents. On the other hand, we were spending more time with them than we ever had; not only did we ride together for several hours every day, we had all our meals together, and after supper we gathered in the living room to listen while Fuzzy read aloud. I particularly remember Macaulay's *History of England* because it went on for so long, and the stories of Damon Runyon, which made Fuzzy laugh so hard he had to put the book down. Another difference was that the atmosphere was jollier, largely because it turned out that Fuzzy could be a lot of fun, even if it was usually at somebody's expense. Still, in my eyes the biggest difference was that Bobby and I could get away, and the minute we did, we could experience everything for ourselves.

Before long we knew everybody on the ranch and had watched them all at work: the foreman Dick Deegan and his family; the cowboy Bob Slocum and his wife, Joyce, who was only sixteen and helped with the laundry; and an aged chore man named Ike who lived alone in a cabin by the shop. There was also George Abbot, our old foreman from Goleta, who had come up with the horses but now mostly did carpentry. And finally, there was William, who was working on the ranch to stay out of the army. William must have had some experience of farm life back in Scotland before he became a butler, because right away Fuzzy put him in charge of the dairy barn and the small herd of Holsteins that supplied the ranch. Morning and evening now he had to milk four or five big black-and-white cows with enormous udders and filthy tails.

Our parents napped every day after lunch, and at three o'clock sharp we would meet at the tack room to saddle up and get ready to ride out. Some days we just checked fences and troughs and salt licks, but mostly we moved cattle from one place to another, slowly so as not to run the fat off them. After the cows were bred, for instance, we had to separate out the great ponderous bulls and drive them back to their own pasture, and very often we looked for cattle that were sick or injured and took them in to the lower corrals to be doctored. Once in, we would push them into the chute, and they would jostle along, nose to tail, to the end, where somebody would clamp the metal frame shut on the one in front so Fuzzy could do the doctoring. Usually, it was simple stuff like wire cuts or infected udders, which he cleaned and painted with gentian blue, but for a while we had an epidemic of pink eye, and I remember day after day bringing in cows with nasty excrescences coming out of their eyelids. As soon as a cow was clamped in place, Fuzzy would grab her by the ear, twist her head round, and shoot puffs of yellow sulfanilamide powder into her eyes. Afterward he would close the lids with his gloved hands and massage them for a bit before releasing her. Then the angry cow would plunge out into the corral, and clang, the frame would shut on the next one.

For cattle work, you need a good horse, and it was a while before everybody got one. The mares that had come up from

**Bobby on Toby, summer 1942**

Goleta were old now, so they were put out to pasture, and my parents bought themselves two lovely grays they named Gazelle and Gazette. Then one day Fuzzy went off and bought a big white-faced strawberry roan called Toby and rode him all the way back to the ranch—thirty miles, I think it was. That horse lay in the dust all the next day, and when he finally got up, Fuzzy took me out on him and told me to canter. I gave the horse a kick, and he put up his head and took off—slam, slam, slam—at a gallop, with me flopping all over, completely out of control and sick with shame. Fuzzy, of course, was disgusted and told Bobby to try him. He handled him fine, so Toby was his. Then Pamela got the bay mare called Grisel

Young Alice on Grenadier, summer 1943

that Mummy had trained to pull the dog cart in Goleta, and eventually my turn came in the form of a sturdy gray gelding named Grenadier. Not only was he smart and smooth-gaited, he turned out to be really good at working cattle, and on top of it all he was wonderfully companionable. I fell in love as only a ten-year-old girl can. I remember it was toward the end of that first summer, and Bobby and I took to going over to the barn in the evening after Fuzzy finished reading to us, to say good night to our horses; then we would climb onto the big haystack and lie there searching the crowded sky for shooting stars. Joy, boundless joy, is the only way to describe it. I was so glad to be alive. I never said anything, though, and now I wonder if Bobby felt as I did. I know Pamela didn't, because she never came with us.

Pamela turned seven in August of that year 1942, I turned eleven, then in September Bobby turned nine, and we went our separate ways to school. He was sent to a boys' school in Santa Barbara called La Loma Feliz, and Pamela and I boarded at the Howard School in Montecito, though she didn't last long. Gas was rationed, so we didn't get back to the ranch all that often, and while we were away it turned cold. Our bunkhouses were unheated, and even though Abbot covered the screens with orange canvas before we got home for Christmas, the only difference as far as I could tell was that we couldn't see out.

Christmas came, and it was unlike any that we had ever experienced. The day was like summer, whereas in Long Island it had always been cold and dark, usually with snow on the ground. There we had always had a tree with lights on it and presents underneath, but now Fuzzy said it was wrong to cut trees down just to decorate the house for a week. Instead, they got out a carved wooden Nativity scene from a place in Germany called Oberammergau, set it up on a table in the living room, and surrounded it with branches from the cedar tree by the garage. In Long Island we had always put up stockings, but this time we were told to leave one of our none-too-clean boots in front of the big stone fireplace. There was no talk of Santa Claus, and in the morning we found that somebody had simply dumped small gifts and fruit into our boots without wrapping anything. Fuzzy had begun saying we were poor (something that my mother must have found rather vulgar, now that I think about it, especially since what money they had was hers), and that was confirmed for me when my main present was a silver bracelet with a heart-shaped lock and I found out that Lizzie Davis got the same thing in her stocking. On the other hand, Christmas was really fun, because other families came in the evening and we sang carols and played all kinds of games. Fuzzy was at his boisterous best, and everyone had a good time.

In fact, my father was boisterous a lot of the time now. He joked around with the men, who called him by his nickname, Duke, and he was constantly teasing us children and tickling us and giving us funny names. Out riding he would sing loudly and off-key. I say "off-key" in both senses of the word, because he was tone-deaf and one song he used to sing began, "She's got pimples on her BUT she's pretty." "Duke, *please*," Mummy would say.

It rained, and at once the ranch turned green, green as Long Island. It didn't rain much or often, but when it did puddles formed in the roads and turned to mud. The trails could get slick in places, and we had to move the cattle slowly and carefully so their hooves wouldn't tear up the grass. The calving season began, and we rode among the cows, checking for those in trouble. I remember seeing mothers wandering about with afterbirth dangling under their dirty tails, while their snowy-faced babies jackknifed themselves up and tottered after them until they found the teats and latched on. The rain made the earth mucky in the spots where the cattle gathered, but at the same time there was more water in the creek, so Bobby and I took to fishing. It was just an idea, because we never caught anything. But then one morning we did catch a pretty big trout, and since we hadn't brought a basket or anything and were both too squeamish to hold that slithery thing, I stuck it headfirst into one of my moccasins and walked all the way back to the house half-barefoot. Then Nancy cooked it and Fuzzy ate it for breakfast.

Spring came, the sun shone all the time again, and now the ranch turned blue and gold from all the lupine and poppies. I'm not sure if we were on vacation or somebody fetched us specially, but when the time came for the branding we were home. First thing that bright, dry morning, friends and neighbors began to appear, some on horseback and others in pickups with trailers, and when everybody was assembled and ready, out we all rode to round up the cattle. The air was cool, and the horses jumped around, but then everybody got to work gathering cattle here and there, pushing them along, picking up strays and adding them to the bunch we were herding. It wasn't difficult: beef cattle are pretty easygoing, and in a few hours the corrals down by Zaca Road were full and teeming. Fuzzy made us children get off and out of the way, so we had to tie up our horses and watch from a fence. The calves were being separated and pushed a few at a time into the main corral, where pairs of riders cantered about on stocky short-coupled horses, chasing steers and whirling their ropes in widening loops. One would drop a loop over the head, dally, and pull his horse back hard onto his haunches to keep the rope taut while the other went for the heels, or the other way round. Then the riders would jump off, wrestle the steer down, and tie him up by the feet. Fuzzy didn't rope— he didn't know how—but he was all over the ground with the others, clipping horns, inoculating, and branding. He would grab a long iron off the fire and press the red-hot end down on the haunch of a calf, then hold it firm until the hide smoked and smelled of burning. In the case of a bull calf, the foreman would step in last thing, seize the squirming calf's testicles in his left hand, and feel around with his thumb to position them. Then a quick slash with his knife and out he would pull them through the slit, cut them off, and toss them into a pail. Somebody else would come with a can of medicine and a paintbrush and paint the bloody place, and in a matter of minutes it was over. The poor creature would be freed to struggle up and join the others, who were huddled at the edge of the corral, bawling, with bright red blood running down the white insides of their legs. The riders meanwhile got back on their horses, coiled their ropes, and trotted off to begin again. When all the calves were done, the foreman splashed some water on his hands, walked over to the barbecue, and grilled all those slimy testicles as well as a bunch of steaks, and everybody sat down at a couple of long tables and ate and drank. The day was still warm and the air was full of dust and the sound of cows and calves bawling when it was time to take our horses and go home. That was our very first branding. The last was forty-six years later, the spring after Mummy died.

We went back to school, and a month or so later Miss Esther Howard came looking for me. She said my mother had had a baby girl and her name was Edith.

I always thought the date was April 18, until one day not all that long ago I spotted a headline in *Vogue* that said, "Happy Birthday, Edie Sedgwick!" The date was April 20, 2015. That's how I learned when her real birthday was, and how I learned to my astonishment that even now, more than forty years after her death, Edie was famous.

I didn't actually see her until I arrived home for the summer, and although it cannot have been my first glimpse, I remember coming upon a screened bed with a lid on it and a diaper over the lid, standing in the sun behind Bobby's bunkhouse. There was nobody around, and Edie was in there, asleep. Even I, who had no use for babies, could see that she was pretty. In fact, from the very beginning Edie stood out among the rest of us. For the first few months she had a trained nurse to look after her, but by the time fall came round that nurse was gone, and a permanent nanny arrived. Her name was Nan Meikle, and she was a big solid Scotswoman, mannish, with red-gold hair, pale skin, and colorless eyes. Although strict, she was good-natured, and unlike Sophie, who kept to herself and never left her charges, she was outspoken and self-assured. She got on with everybody, from Fuzzy to William and Nancy, and soon became part of the rowdy poker game that now floated between our kitchen and the foreman's house.

Nan Meikle proved to have strict views about toilet training. She was shocked to find Edie still in diapers at the age of six months, and she wasn't going to have it. She made Edie sit on the potty until she "did something," as she put it. She said, "You hold them up, the little potty on your lap, and then patiently wait. It doesn't take them very long to know what they're there for." Only Nan could have managed to train Edie like that, because even as a very small child she didn't like to be told what to do. She had winning ways—Mummy's word for her was "beguiling"—but she was headstrong: right from the start she wanted her way and she got it. To one degree or another, the rest of us were afraid of our parents and alarmed by the least sign of disapproval, but not Edie; Edie defied them. Now, I had defied them too when I was small. I remember at Goleta once when I was about three, I ran away from Mummy and the nurse and locked myself in a bathroom. Fuzzy came and shouted through the door, but I didn't open it (I can still see the knob and the lock, which were at my eye level), and next thing I knew he burst in through the window, high up over the tub, and came after me. Not only did I get a terrific walloping, the episode was held up from then on as evidence of my bad character. But when Edie defied them, nothing happened. Nothing. Nan said, "Edie had a will of her own. It was born in her. The parents spoilt her. Anything Edie wanted to do was fine with her parents, but not with me. She had to mind and she had to eat everything on her plate." But if there was something Edie did want, she carried on until she

38

got it, and then she threw herself into it. What she loved best from the very beginning was horses and everything to do with them. She was only fourteen months old when Mummy put her in the saddle for the first time. And when she was nineteen months old, in January 1945, Mummy had another baby, another girl, named Susanna but called Suky.

Edie's full name was Edith Minturn, after Fuzzy's beautiful aunt who was married to the architect and reformer Isaac Newton Phelps Stokes; the two of them are the subjects of that

Sedgwick family, eight children, spring 1945

39

lovely Sargent double portrait in the Metropolitan Museum in New York. Suky was named for Fuzzy's formidable grandmother Susanna Shaw Minturn, and she was as fair as Edie was dark, with round blue eyes and hair like a dandelion seed. That made three girls in a row, eight children in all, and after that there were no more babies.

Our grandfather Babbo had been living with us right along, but he had his own life, completely separate from ours. He was in his early eighties then, slightly bent so that he walked with a stick, and distinguished-looking, with short white hair parted in the middle. Every day he dressed in exactly the same way, in a white shirt, plain woolen tie, gray herringbone tweed coat and waistcoat, and knickerbockers with colored socks and big old shoes, well shined. He followed the same routine every day too, rising early—we could hear him in the bathroom, stropping his straight razor and cussing if he cut himself—and withdrawing after breakfast to the little study off the front hall where he spent his days. He was writing a book about a French lady called Madame de Tencin, who he explained lived in the eighteenth century and kept a salon. (He never finished that one, but a couple of years later he wrote a book about Horace that was his last, because then he fell in love and got married.) Around four in the afternoon he would rise from his desk, put his tattered Harvard football sweater over his shoulders and his old gray fedora on his head, and stump out the door. All the dogs on the ranch would be waiting, and off he would go, down the road as far as the pigs, with dogs bounding about in all directions. Babbo loved the landscape and all the animals—I remember he had a favorite bull he called Paul Potter—but he took no part in what went on at the ranch. Even at the table he was generally quiet in the presence of our parents, whose conversation was confined to practical matters and remonstrations directed at us children. He was affectionate with Fuzzy, calling him "Sonny," but Fuzzy was oddly formal with him, and Mummy was even more so. I know Babbo worried about bothering her because he didn't ask her to cut his hair. Instead, he asked me, and he was never cross at the result.

My mother was as good as a real barber, because Fuzzy had made her learn how before they got married, and she had all the professional equipment. She cut his hair and everybody else's in the family except Babbo's and mine. (I had to go with her to the hairdresser and have a permanent, same as she did.) What amazes me as I think about her now and realize that she was only in her thirties in those years, is how unbelievably competent my mother was, managing that large and various household. I remember seeing lists in her tidy handwriting in the kitchen or by the phone in the hall, because she would work out the menus for the week with Nancy, two big meals a day plus breakfast, which was another big meal, for up to sixteen people, not counting guests, and then she would order everything over the telephone, and the orders always had to be picked up. In all this, if my father was along he never even unloaded the car; he left it all to her and whatever children were around. And it wasn't only groceries she had to think about; there were prescriptions to be ordered and fetched, things to buy at the hardware store, stuff to drop off or pick up at the repairman's or the cleaners, then there were clothes, shoes, boots for us children, and on top of that there were all the appointments—doctors and dentists and allergists and

other specialists—plus dogs to go to the vet and people need-
ing to be taken places—Babbo to the library, me to my friend
Lavinia's house, every kind of miscellaneous errand. And then
there were the emergencies. One time Bobby was racing in
the bull pasture with a cousin, and when he looked back his
horse took him under a tree and slammed him into a branch
so hard he got a concussion and had to spend the night in the
hospital; and another time Pamela got kicked in the head just
above her right eye and Mummy had to drive her all the way
to Santa Barbara to the emergency room while Bobby held the
gruesome wound together and they didn't know whether Pamela would be able to see out of that eye. In short, it was endless, and my mother took care of it all. Not only that, she did
it so matter-of-factly that nobody noticed. Absolutely nothing
threw her until, all those years later, she had to put Edie in the
mental hospital. I think that was the only time I ever heard
her cry.

She was shy now, and uncomfortable at parties, but it
never occurred to me to connect it with her looks, her smile
that pulled around to the side. Where she was happiest was at
home on the ranch. She no longer played the piano, because
Fuzzy said it took too much time away from the children, but
she listened to music by herself for hours every morning, and
every afternoon she was out working cattle. In between, she
dealt with whatever was necessary. And to my shame, all my
adult life I would tell people I never saw my mother lift a finger except to saddle her horse. True, she never held a job, she
didn't take care of the children, she certainly never cleaned,
and she couldn't do the least thing in the kitchen: one time
she almost cut her thumb off trying to open a can.

Fuzzy was the one who didn't work. That is, he did the daily cattle work, but he didn't run the ranch. The foreman, Dick Deegan, did that, and Fuzzy left him to it until eventually it was discovered that Dick had been embezzling. That was a big shock—he was such a likeable guy, and Fuzzy hated having to fire him. But pretty soon we had a new foreman, called L. D. McVeigh, Dee for short, and he was with us from then on, fifty years in all. Fuzzy loved and trusted Dee, and I doubt if he ever gave another thought to the management of the ranch. So I suppose you would say he was a gentleman rancher, although by profession, he was a sculptor.

My father was the youngest of three boys. As a child he was frail and sickly, full of fears, and he never reached six feet, whereas his brothers Harry and Minturn were both six-four, and by the time Fuzzy entered Groton School, Minturn was on his way to becoming a nationally famous athlete. I don't think my father even played varsity sports in college, but from an early age he did everything he could to build up and perfect his body.

As a young man he was so overweeningly ambitious, so consumed by the idea of fame, that his uncle Ellery Sedgwick thought his parents had cause for alarm. He started out as a banker, working for Lazard Frères in London, but he broke down and was taken in by the de Forests, who had rented a house in England for the shooting season. I asked Grandma once how that came about, and she said he was their son Charley's school friend and they knew the family; however, Mummy was there too, and it was during that time that Fuzzy proposed. Then after they were married, he got another job and they went to Germany, but something must have happened in that case as well, because by the time I came along, his profession was sculpture. He practiced it all his life except at Corral de Quati, where he didn't have a studio. He worked entirely in the academic tradition, and since he had a gift for capturing likenesses, for a long time he specialized in portrait busts. He made monuments and religious images as well, and in the late fifties he began to work on an equestrian statue of a cowboy, the one he finally developed into the large monument that stands in Earl Warren Park in Santa Barbara. In a way, my father's career was not unlike his own father's, because Babbo started out as a lawyer in New York, but he found the law uncongenial, and as soon as he married he gave it up to become a scholar. He was so successful as a popular historian that until recently his name, Henry Dwight Sedgwick, was in the *Columbia Encyclopedia*, along with that of his brother Ellery, the longtime editor of *The Atlantic Monthly*. Fuzzy, however, didn't think his father was successful because he never made any money. Babbo didn't mind. He loved his scholarly life, and he never had the slightest interest in being grand.

To us children, our grandfather's company was pure enchantment. Whenever our parents were absent at mealtimes, he would take over and regale us with tales of Baron Munchausen and his outrageous lies or, sometimes, the miracles of his personal protector, Saint Exupère. The principal job of this beloved saint was to find whatever my grandfather mislaid, but he had also been known to cure a toothache, and once he even produced somebody out of an empty landscape to change a flat tire. However, what strikes me now as odd is that we never heard any stories about Babbo's own life or the history of the Sedgwick family. It was only many decades later, when I chanced upon his memoirs in a rented house in northern Italy, that I learned that my own grandfather could remember a boy running up the village street in Stockbridge, Massachusetts, shouting that Lincoln had been shot, and what's more, that he was out in the streets of New York during the Great Blizzard of '88, he saw Eleonora Duse onstage, and he knew and didn't particularly like Henry James. More surprisingly, although he was born and raised there, he never once mentioned the village of Stockbridge or the big house on Main Street that his ancestor Judge Theodore Sedgwick built. He never said that Judge Sedgwick had been Speaker of the House under Jefferson or that he'd won the freedom of a slave named Mumbet in a famous case that led directly to the abolition of slavery in Massachusetts. I suppose he was brought up not to talk about anything personal, because that's how we were brought up too, and now as I write all this I am uncomfortably aware that the mere recitation of facts like these can amount to bragging.

My grandfather never talked about the war, but at noon every day he would pull a chair up to the big radio in the living room and sit hunched over with his hands cupping his ears so he could listen to the news. No one else did that, and nobody said much about the war, not when thin blue letters came from Uncle Minturn in London, not even when two of Fuzzy's closest friends were killed in action and he took their deaths so very hard. The only time I remember everybody talking about it was that spring after Suky was born, when the Germans surrendered and it felt as if the war was over, or about to be.

Meanwhile, it turned out that Fuzzy had written a novel. It was called *The Rim*, it came out in April of that year, and even at the age of thirteen I could tell that it was autobiographical. It was about a sculptor whose name was Robert (Uncle Minturn's first name) Suffren (*S* like Sedgwick, sounds like "suffering"), who marries a perfectly nice woman called Catherine. She adores him, but as time goes on he finds her less and less attractive, so he falls in love with somebody named Martha, who has a boring husband and a couple of children. (The summer before at Goleta, Bobby and I had noticed Fuzzy up by the pool talking privately and with great intensity to a woman friend of theirs; pretty soon we heard that her husband had up and moved the whole family away.) He and Martha make love (I was really interested in that part, but the way it was described—"Their mating was as natural as the elements," I think was the phrase—was uninformative, to say the least), and in the end they give each other up nobly, and Catherine dies in childbirth, I can't remember in which order. As it happened, my mother was away in the East when the book came out, and one day as I was looking in the desk for an envelope I came upon a letter from her telling him what she thought of it. (Hold on! He never showed her what he was writing?) The letter was restrained in tone, and the sentence that stuck in my mind was this: "I find aspects of myself in the unfortunate Catherine." I put it back very carefully and didn't mention it or the book or anything to do with it to anybody.

I was shocked and unsettled. I knew this meant something about my parents' relationship, but it didn't occur to me to question their marriage; they were just two aspects of the same thing. They had everything in common—background, values, and preferences—and they both enjoyed the fact that their personalities were opposite but complementary. Mainly, they both loved everything about life on the ranch. All that was on the bright side, the side everybody saw. On the dark side there was something else they had in common, something I never heard either of my parents mention: both of them were the youngest of four, and in each of their families half the children had died young. My mother's brother Henry died of a brain tumor when he was ten and she was three; and before my father was born, his parents lost an infant daughter whose name was Edith Minturn Sedgwick. (She was never mentioned; all I heard was that Edie was named for Fuzzy's beautiful aunt.) Some years went by, and first my father's family and then my mother's was stricken again: his brother Harry died of pneumonia in his last year at Groton School, and Charley de Forest died of a fever while traveling in Italy in the fall of 1929, months after my parents married. The families were shattered, and their grief was terrible. So my mother and father knew all along that it could happen, children could die, they just never spoke of it. We were the ones who didn't know.

Nobody seemed to be talking about Fuzzy's book and what it seemed to suggest. Life went on as usual until one morning I walked into the house and there was the paper, the *Santa Barbara News-Press*, announcing that an American plane had dropped an atomic bomb on the city of Hiroshima in Japan and the whole entire city and everybody in it and for miles around was destroyed. It was August 6, 1945. On the twenty-ninth I turned fourteen, on September 2 the war was over, and right after that I went away to a real girls' boarding school.

# III

The Katherine Branson School was and still is in Marin County, outside San Francisco, four hundred miles away, and my parents drove me there the first time instead of putting me on the train. My suitcase was full of blue-and-white uniforms, hand-me-downs from somebody who had decided not to go back, but I arrived in my own new clothes: plain blouse and good gray skirt, cotton stockings the color of cocoa held up by my first panty girdle, and low-heeled shoes. On top of that I was wearing a bulky aquamarine-colored overcoat with shoulder pads, plus a matching fedora hat with a feather. My mother had chosen that outfit specially for my new circumstances, but since Fuzzy had been saying we were poor, I took it as a sign of our poverty when I saw how the other girls were dressed. However, it turned out that the only thing my new schoolmates noticed about me was my handsome father, so I was perfectly happy to put on my uniform and settle in among them.

Some of the girls proved to be clothes-conscious after all, but in a way that had to do with fashion, and that was new to me because in my family dress had exclusively to do with codes of class. According to my mother, a woman's appearance ought to reflect the person she was, meaning she should look like a lady and be consistent in her style. Away from the ranch, she herself always dressed in an austere and practical manner, in plain colors, never in anything remotely either feminine or fashionable. What jewelry she wore was discreet, and although she would apply a touch of lipstick if she was going anywhere, she kept her nails short and would not have dreamt of painting them. I had observed that Grandma and all my mother's friends in the East dressed according to this same code, except that some women were really elegant and some even wore lots of lipstick and painted their long and shapely nails dark red to match. Here in California, however, most of the women we knew appeared in bright colors and amazing textures and great big jewelry, and in summer instead of spectator pumps they wore sandals that revealed their perfect tan feet and bright toenails. They smoked, and to me their accoutrements—cigarette cases inlaid with lapis lazuli and jade, enameled holders, and gold monogrammed lighters with tops that flicked up—were the very essence of glamour. I thought everything about these women was glamorous, but my mother made it clear that such gaudiness was not for us, and she dressed me as severely as she dressed herself. She softened somewhat with her other daughters as the years went by, and when it came to Edie, she wound up buying her whatever she wanted, even when her taste ran to things I thought made her look pretty cheap.

I imagine that Edie too longed for feminine clothes, particularly because in the early years at Corral de Quati, she and Suky and Kate were dressed identically in little corduroy overalls and jackets, hand-me-downs from some other large family. I personally thought they looked nice, all dressed alike even though they were so very different. Some families look like suits of cards, but we were all different, and we had very different temperaments and interests. That was particularly true of the little girls, although all three really loved to ride. Kate, who was always tall for her age, had brown eyes and curly blond hair that she wore in braids. She was bighearted and boisterous, and of us all she was the most gregarious. Edie had dark shiny eyes and hair and rosy cheeks with dimples, and while she was pretty and captivating, she wanted her way and she could be mean; her passions were horses and drawing. And as for Suky, she was not like anyone else. She had sky-blue eyes and short flyaway hair that was almost white, and she went about the world in a daze of wonder. Even as an infant in Nan Meikle's arms she would bounce and crow at the least sound of music. Pamela and I were also musical, but otherwise, we could not have been more different. She was a lovely-looking child with dark hair and a pale oval face, and of us all she was the only one who never really took to ranch life. She missed Long Island, where she had worn pretty dresses and Sophie tied ribbons in her hair, whereas to me life at Corral de Quati was heaven on earth. I read poetry and cowboy romances and dreamt of a future in a wild landscape. The fact that we were not supposed to care about looks was fine with me, because unlike the rest of the family I was rather stocky and nondescript-looking, and Fuzzy was always on my case for being fat.

In California the boys rarely needed their good clothes, but these too were a matter of East Coast convention and class: short pants and jackets without lapels to the age of twelve, and thereafter, long trousers and lapels on the jackets. All three of my brothers were handsome. Bobby had dark eyes and straight dark hair, and for a long time he was bashful and hung his head if a grown-up looked at him. He was tough, though. By the time he was ten he was driving the big army surplus truck, and he had a series of guns: air rifles and

BB guns, and eventually a twenty-two with which he liked to hunt the bobcats that crouched in the live oaks, looking to drop onto the calves. Minty was the middle son and Fuzzy's namesake; he too had guns, although by nature he was the gentlest of us all. He had large brown eyes and light brown curly hair, and the most endearing smile you ever saw; you could tell he was eager to please. Everyone admired the cowboy comics he drew, which were always filled with *POWs* and *ZOWIEs* and sprays of stars denoting violence. Jonathan was blond with brown eyes, he stood erect and looked straight out at the world, and he was really capable. I think he was thirteen when he built a handsome room onto the boys' bunkhouse, with real windows and built-in bunks with lockers below.

The main issue regarding the boys was not their appearance but manliness. It was always on my father's mind. He loved to show off his muscular body, and he was inordinately proud of the thick dark hair he had on his head and all over his back and chest. So he kept after the boys, especially out riding, even though they all rode well. Bobby in particular was aggressive to the point of foolhardiness, and he was apt to have accidents. Jonathan was brave too, but sensible, and he seldom got into trouble. Minty, however, was fearful, so Fuzzy came down hardest on him, always calling him an old woman and a sissy.

Much as I missed the ranch, I can't say I was ever homesick after I got to school, and one reason was that at school I had nothing to fear. The rules were entirely reasonable, whereas at home the system was both despotic and quite unpredictable. Years later Bobby and I would call it a fascist regime and joke about the ministries of labor, information, and justice, but at the time it was no joke. In fairness, the labor part was just chores, but the restriction of information was not normal, and its effects were lasting. Growing up, we never knew what was happening or where we were going or what was planned for us, and not only were we never consulted, we were not allowed to ask. Everything came as a bolt from the blue; nothing was ever explained, so we had difficulty knowing what was what. As for the justice system, it was harsh, and since I was heedless, I was constantly falling afoul of it. However, I was the exception among the girls, because Pamela was careful to stay out of trouble, Kate and Suky were naturally good, and Edie was always special, whatever she did. She was the only one Fuzzy never spanked.

In any case, we each had a different experience of life in the family, and as things changed over time, the younger children's was very different from mine. That was especially true of the little girls, first of all because the ranch was all they knew, and second because for years they lived apart from the rest of us. Here's how that came about: during my first year away at school Abbot made a girls' bunkhouse for Pamela and me out of my old one and the chore man's cabin, which had real windows and a bathroom (I was devastated), and the following year he built one for the three boys by attaching Bobby's and Pamela's old bunkhouses at either side of a brand-new room. Then Abbot fell ill and died, and next thing you know, our parents moved Sophie and the three little girls into his cottage. So now there were no children left in the main house, and the youngest were the ones who lived farthest away. I still don't understand. Babbo had already moved back east, so what did they want with all those empty bedrooms? If it was for guests, why not put them in Abbot's house?

The cottage stood at some distance from the main house, and it was good-sized, with a living room, a dining room, and several bedrooms; and with Mrs. Abbot there to do the cooking, it was completely self-sufficient. Moreover, it had a large fenced yard, so it was as if Sophie and the little girls now lived in a big pen, like something out of *Mother Goose*. I know my mother went over there to see the children and take them riding and to the doctor and all that, but I can't imagine that Fuzzy went very often if at all—much as he enjoyed them later on, he never had the faintest interest in children under the age of eight or nine. I went over there, not so much to visit Sophie or my siblings as to talk to Joyce, the cowboy's wife, who was there doing laundry and who was not that much older than I was. She told me all about her life on the streets in Tijuana, which was how she met her husband.

The other big change that took place around then was the school. My mother had been getting packets of workbooks and stuff from a place in Baltimore called the Calvert Method, and I guess she struggled through several years with the help of a lady named Miss Jacobs, until Jonathan failed first grade. Then Fuzzy sent a telegram to a couple he had known in New York to see if they would come and start a school on the ranch. How he guessed that this would appeal to them I have no idea—Vic Bryant was a musician, and while he was at Juilliard his wife had modeled for artists, which is how Fuzzy knew them—but a telegram came straight back saying "YES" ten times. No signature or anything, just ten yeses in capital letters. So a house was fixed up for them and for the school on the other side of the cottage, and in due course the Bryant family appeared. They were all tall and long-legged, even the two children, who were the ages of Jonathan and Kate. It turned out to be a perfect match and a great success all round. Children came from other ranches nearby and the school thrived. After a couple of years, Vic went to teach at Midland School over on the other side of Los Olivos, so Minty had to ride his horse many miles cross-country every week for his clarinet lesson.

The ranch school must have been pretty good, because everybody got into boarding school: the girls followed me to

Minty on Donatello, ca. 1947

Branson's, and the boys followed Bobby to Groton. That was the main thing, because in our family there was only one school that mattered, and it was Groton. Groton was where you were supposed to play football and make the friends who would continue with you to Harvard and on through your whole life. It was an Episcopalian school, founded by a minister everybody called the Rector, although his real name was Endicott Peabody, and Babbo's brother Ellery had been the first member of the family to go there—class of 1890. When Fuzzy entered, however, the school must have had distressing associations for him, because his elder brother Harry had died there of pneumonia only a couple of years before. On the other hand, Fuzzy's middle brother, Uncle Minturn, had not only been a legendary football player, he had also fallen in love and was bent on marrying the Rector's daughter Helen. In fact, Fuzzy too could have met his future wife there, given that Mummy's brother Charley de Forest was in his class, but instead they met in Santa Barbara, because my father didn't stay at Groton. What happened was that his mother, who had been failing since Harry's death, suddenly had a stroke and within a few days she was dead. They got Fuzzy there in time to see her, and that was too much; he broke down and had to be taken out of school. He was fourteen years old. The Rector advised Babbo to send him out west, which is what they did in those days if you were not robust: they sent you out to Arizona or California for the climate. So that's how my father wound up at the Cate School in Carpinteria, California, and it turned out to be the ideal place for him. It was set in beautiful country not far from the coast, the boys all had their own horses, and the headmaster and his wife took him in and treated him as a member of their family for as long as they lived. He thrived—who wouldn't?—and by the time my mother met him he must have looked pretty terrific. She was fourteen years old, visiting Santa Barbara with her family; he was eighteen, handsome, gregarious, and full of vitality. And that was that: she fell in love for life.

So right at the beginning the precedent was set: California was where my father was healthy and strong, where he flourished and the two of them felt free, where they could live in the light. It was the ideal world, and the East, in contrast, was laden with dark and stern realities. No wonder when I was small the myth of Persephone reminded me of the difference between California and Long Island.

I'm sure my father was far happier at Cate, but all the same, in our universe Groton was the school, just as Harvard was the college, and at Harvard the Porcellian was the club. Sedgwicks had belonged to it since 1813. Fuzzy actually did really well in college—he graduated in three years magna cum laude and won a fellowship to Trinity College, Cambridge—but to hear him talk, you'd think the Porc had been the whole point of college life. There were pigs all over the place wherever we lived, everything from the wooden salt and pepper shakers on the table to a radiator cap on which a large silver pig sat upright, tootling on a double pipe. That pig adorned every car my father drove from the time I was small until they stopped making cars that required radiator caps. Clubs mattered a lot in life, that was clear, and the Porcellian was only the first. In New York alone my father belonged to the River Club, the Racquet Club, the Harvard Club, the Century, and his favorite, the Knickerbocker. When he went to Boston there was the Somerset, and in San Francisco, the Pacific Union. If both parents went east, they always stayed at the River Club, but if they went alone Fuzzy stayed at the Knickerbocker, and after Grandma died, my mother joined the Colony. My grandmother told me once that she had never in her life touched her bare feet to the ground, not even in her own room or on the beach, and to me that was the idea about staying in clubs: you never had to touch your feet to the common ground. As I understood it, those institutions were a big part of the world that we were expected, somehow eventually, if we measured up, to inhabit. You could generally tell who measured up just by their presence and their speech. Apparently, another way to tell was by the *Social Register*, or the "stud book," as Fuzzy called it, which was a black hardcover volume with orange lettering that came twice a year in the mail. You could look up your friends' addresses, as well as their college classes, their wives' maiden names, and the names of their children, the assumption being that the people you knew would be in it. One way you knew that somebody might not measure up was if Fuzzy said they "didn't come from the top drawer." His snobbishness was selective, however; it applied only to the East and not at all in California. The real snob was Grandma, who considered the *Social Register* vulgar. She also looked down upon the DAR and all women's clubs that were not the Colony, and she thought it odd that I should have a friend with Vanderbilt blood. But she was a lady, so she was discreet about her opinions, and my mother was the same.

Everybody could see what a lady my mother was, and one effect was that nobody on or around the ranch in those days called her by her first name; except to her close friends, she was always Mrs. Sedgwick. Moreover, she herself made it clear that it was important to be perceived as a lady. One time she and I were in the post office in Santa Barbara—I must have been fifteen—and a young clerk called me "Baby." I was flattered, but on the way out Mummy said sharply, "He could see that you're not a lady." So: being a lady gave you control over the way others behaved toward you, it kept them in their place, and it also gave you that death-ray power of disapproval. It's not that I didn't know the technique: you had to display the signals and make sure they registered, all the while acting very gracious. I simply couldn't do it. I wish I could say I was rebelling; no, I was just eager to please, and I certainly didn't think of myself as a lady. Anyway, so long as I was on the ranch or at school I didn't have to worry about it. Nevertheless, it appears I had one marker, because not long after she arrived at Branson's, a younger girl called Jean Stein introduced me to her parents, and she told me decades later that her mother had said she should get to know me and learn to speak as I did. By the way, I don't imagine there were too many Jewish boys at Groton when my brothers were there, but at Branson's, Jean and her little sister were not the only Jewish girls, and I became aware of an uncomfortable difference, something that set them apart. Not that it seemed to concern the Stein sisters, who were at once exotic and very confident. They both had little black dresses from Dior, and whereas I kept snapshots of my family and my horse on my bureau, Jean had a picture of the future Aga Khan and his brother on a beach in the south of France. However, I still remember a classmate explaining with anguish what it meant to her to play the part of Shylock, and I remember the intensity of her performance. It seemed that even being Catholic was a problem in some families: girls were always asking whether your parents would let you marry one. Questions like that were never raised in my family; the subject simply didn't come up.

Branson's was an absolutely wonderful school, as anyone who has read Julia Child's biography will know: she said it changed her life, and it certainly changed mine. It was Episcopalian—meaning church every Sunday and grace before meals—and nobody would have called it progressive, but Miss Branson and the small cohort of other spinsters who came west with her from Bryn Mawr to found it were high-minded. You could sense it in the everyday life of the school, in its standards and traditions, and in the experiences that were made available to us. The school had a rich library and a large collection of records of classical music, on both of which I feasted, plus there were all sorts of interesting extracurricular programs to choose from. In addition, we were taken regularly to museums in San Francisco, and those of us who were musical received tickets to the symphony and the opera and concerts of every kind. In addition, special visitors were invited throughout the year to perform for us or to address the student body. So for several years in a row a distinguished Black philosopher and theologian came to lecture to us. His name was Howard Thurman, and Miss Branson treated him with particular deference. He and his equally dignified wife would stay to lunch with her at the head table, and deserving girls would be invited to join them. Years later I learned that Howard Thurman was Martin Luther King Jr.'s mentor and the person who introduced him to Gandhi's theory of radical nonviolence.

But meanwhile, one day during vacation we were all out riding—I remember we were in the Bowl pasture, at the top of a huge wash, with a view of half the world—and Fuzzy got onto the subject of Black people. I suppose I argued with him, because I can tell you exactly what he said. In a tone that meant *That's it, end of discussion*, he said, "It is a well-known fact that the Negro is first cousin to the monkey."

I was married and living in Cambridge in February 1957 when a letter went out under the Groton School letterhead to all alumni and everybody associated with the school, announcing that Groton, which had just admitted its first Black student, would now admit Negro boys in sufficient numbers to make up between a fourth and a third of the total enrollment, and pledging the full use of the school's endowment fund for scholarships. The letter was a hoax, and it created a furor. It was even in the *New York Times*. Weeks went by, and everybody was talking about it and guessing who might have done such a shocking thing. Then one morning my cousin Alexander came to see me, bringing another cousin with him, and the two of them just stood there looking down until finally Alec said, "They know who wrote that Groton letter. It was your father."

But that was still a decade away, and meanwhile, life on the ranch went on as usual. There were so many of us now that we couldn't do much together as a family, other than the

Duke Sedgwick with Edie by the pool in Goleta, ca. 1946

occasional picnic, and we certainly didn't travel. However, as soon as the war was over we began spending weekends in Goleta, where everybody swam and played tennis and friends would come over, so there were always guests at lunch and dinner; and when we went to Santa Barbara, Fuzzy would take whoever was in the car to lunch at a Mexican place on Chapala Street called Pete's, which I think still exists. We always had the big table in the middle, and Pete would come out and joke around with Fuzzy, so it was all very jolly. Plus, on Sunday nights when Nancy was off playing poker, everybody who was old enough would get to go out to dinner at Mattei's Tavern in Los Olivos, and my parents would sing in the car on the way there, but that was about it. The one trip that I recall was the summer of my junior year in school, when my mother packed Bobby and Pamela and me, along with Joe McElroy (the same Joseph McElroy who grew up to become a distinguished writer), who was supposedly tutoring Bobby that summer, into her big 1935 Cadillac touring car and drove us all to Williams, Arizona. We were going to spend a week or so at the Quarter Circle Double X Ranch with the family of Isabella Greenway, a beloved family friend who had died a few years earlier. I remembered her well because she had visited us often at Goleta, and now I learned that she had been the first woman from Arizona to serve in the House of Representatives and a great friend of President Roosevelt. What made the biggest impression on me about her ranch, apart from its vastness and the sparsity of the cattle in that arid landscape, was the nasty three-holer outhouse we had to use, and the fact that FDR had had to be carried out there every time he needed to go.

By then I was used to traveling by myself, because as soon as the war was over my parents had begun sending me east every summer to stay with my grandmother and my Sedgwick and Duer cousins. Somehow, life in the West didn't seem to count in their minds; real life, it was understood, took place in the East, and we were expected to fit in there and do well. So every year from the age of fourteen, I would take the train east and spend several luxurious weeks with Grandma, being thoroughly spoiled, before being taken to visit my cousins at their summer places, Duers in Castine, Maine, and Sedgwicks in Murray Bay on the Saint Lawrence River in Canada. I loved my cousins, I enjoyed the lives they led, and I absolutely adored my grandmother, so for the first couple of summers I was happy enough, although I would always have preferred to be on the ranch. But then I began to feel uneasy because I foresaw that I was going to have to "come out." I regarded it as the test that would reveal that I didn't measure up in the world that mattered to my parents, and not only was I terrified, I had not the faintest interest in any of it. (In the event, I needn't have worried. At the end of my freshman year, Grandma gave a beautiful dinner dance for my cousin Mary Duer and me, with a tent on the lawn and a Lester Lanin band in the drawing room and flowers everywhere. All my Sedgwick cousins came, and I got to invite some of my friends from college, and that was all there was to it, except that the date was June 25, 1950. By the time we went to bed we knew that America had declared war on North Korea, and the boys were facing the draft. It was the only debutante party I ever went to.)

At home, however, nobody mentioned the subject of coming out. Instead, Fuzzy talked a lot about marriage. What he said, and he said so over and over, was that girls to be successful had to marry young, ideally at nineteen, but if not then, the sooner the better, that was the main thing. Then he would say that however desirable a suitor might be, however much you loved him, you had to put him to the test by saying no the first two times he proposed. Neither he nor my mother seemed to feel that education mattered for a girl, and there was never any talk of working or a career: marriage was the goal. The result was that of the five girls, only two of us went to college, and I am the only one to have worked most of my life. And of the five of us, only Pamela followed Fuzzy's prescription. She went to Smith for one year, and then, at the precise age of nineteen, she married the older brother of her best friend. Not only was he extremely handsome, with fine features and hair the color of burnished copper, he had gone to Groton and was planning to go back to Harvard as soon as he got out of the army. Plus, he was really nice.

I don't know whose idea it was, but Pamela, who had done very well at Branson's, had transferred to a girls' school in Maryland called St. Timothy's for her senior year, and she was so well liked and successful there that she was elected president of her class. That's how she met her best friend and a number of other really nice girls from old families on the East Coast, all of whom began coming out to the ranch. They loved it—who wouldn't?—and my parents loved having them. They were bridesmaids in Pamela's wedding, and her best friend was maid of honor. And for the rest of her life, I was told many years later, every time Pamela went to New York, her friends would be excited to see her, and somebody would give a party. That's the way it was all supposed to be, and it's certainly what our parents had in mind for Edie when they sent her to live in Cambridge. I'm sure they imagined she would meet a nice Harvard boy from a family they knew, and she would get married and everything would be just fine. It's also what Edie meant when she would tell interviewers that she was looking for another way, different from the way of her parents.

## IV

My own transition from the ranch to a life of my own was not so smooth, putting it mildly, and I was over thirty when I finally found my way. I did well enough at Branson's to get into Radcliffe, which I chose because I thought it was Harvard and I was expecting the Athenian stoa. But meanwhile, I received the most unexpected and utterly miraculous gift of my entire life: my parents sent me to Europe for the summer with a cousin. We sailed from New York on a battered little Greek steamer called the *Neptunia*, and from the moment we arrived in the bay of Naples amid a blazing sunset to the moment we took off from London airport in the rain to fly home, I was in heaven. I landed back in New York convinced that I had entered the real world and that it was going to be all I had imagined.

I cannot remember who if anyone accompanied me to Cambridge, but I arrived at Radcliffe in time for orientation. Actually, "disorientation" would have been a better word, because right away I could tell that I did not have the key to the map on which I found myself. To begin with, although my dorm was a conventional enough brick building, dark inside and rather dingy, the girls I encountered there were like nobody I had ever seen, they were so unbelievably smart and accomplished. Just to give you a small idea, there was one girl who had played a Mozart concerto with some big orchestra in New York, and another who was trying to crack Linear B and kept shoeboxes full of file cards under her bed, and most extraordinary of all, there was a big jovial girl by the name of

Martha Fontek who could take a passage of Chaucer, translate it into French at sight, and recite it backward. Then there were some gay girls, as well as a freshman who looked just like Wolf Gal in *Li'l Abner* and who told a wide-eyed group of us that yes, sure, she had slept with boys and it was wonderful. And here is just a sample of the references and topics of conversation that I had never heard of: Raskolnikov, Unamuno, alienation, "red-diaper babies" (of which there were a bunch in my dorm), and of course, Senator McCarthy and the House Un-American Activities Committee. Everyone was angry and alarmed about what was going on there. When I went home for Christmas I asked Fuzzy, and he said it had to be done somehow, we had to get rid of the Communists. And when I mentioned the subject to my grandmother, she was uncomfortable, because my cousin Beverley Duer had told her I was a pinko.

Not surprisingly, I was completely at a loss in class as well. I was used to learning by rote—e.g., conjugations and declensions and kings and wars—and here I had to take courses in which I was presented with a series of seemingly disparate texts, such as Plutarch's *Life of Alcibiades*, *Henry IV, Part I*, and *The Education of Henry Adams*, and expected to draw some conclusions. Then there was the social landscape: I had almost never in my life been on a date, so now of course I went out with anyone who asked me—football players and premeds and shy intellectuals and clubbies who got drunk and cocky guys on the make—and from afar I glimpsed what I had been half dreading, the young gods who came out of boarding schools like Exeter and had everything, including girlfriends who were their exact counterparts.

It turned out I had a number of cousins at Harvard as well

as uncles and aunts and cousins in and around Boston, all of whom were wonderfully welcoming. Uncle Minturn would ask me regularly to Sunday lunch at his big white house in Dedham, where my grandfather was living now, so I would see him and various cousins, and everyone would wonder about Babbo behind his back, because he had fallen in love and was courting a beautiful and cultivated lady in her forties. (He married her in 1953 and had four years of cloudless happiness before he died.) Then from time to time my great-uncle Ellery Sedgwick would invite me out to Beverly on the North Shore, where he lived in a fine Georgian house called Long Hill that was famous for its gardens. My relatives were kind and delightful, and I have loved them all ever since, but there was no bridging the abyss between their ways of life and life in the dorm, where so much was bewildering and terrible things went on. In my first term a girl tried to kill herself and was carried away half-dead on a stretcher, and soon after that the brother of somebody's boyfriend went to prison for taking a girl to Cape Cod to get an abortion that went wrong. He wasn't even the baby's father; he was just trying to help.

Aside from everything else, I had no idea how to do the most ordinary things. I had never taken public transportation, I had never had a checkbook, I had never consulted a schedule or made an appointment. Moreover, having been strictly trained to believe that others knew better than I did, I was incapable of figuring anything out. I mention all this because if it was true of me, it must have been all the more true of Edie when her turn came to leave the ranch, because the isolation in which we were raised only increased over the years, and in her case it was total.

I blundered about trying this and that and making dubious choices until the middle of my sophomore year, when I got engaged to a serious Jewish guy at the law school, the first veteran I had ever met and the first Marxist, whom I looked up to and learned from but did not love, and who had persuaded me to sleep with him. I went home for Christmas vacation and admitted to my parents that I did not want to get married. To my surprise, they were calm. Nothing was said, and after Christmas they took me to Florence and left me there with relations of old family friends. I stayed for a year and a half, having a beautiful time, making friends that I have had ever since, and learning a certain amount that served me well both immediately, because of the courses I was now competent to take, and in the long run because it determined my working life. I came home in the summer of 1951, still pretty clueless but convinced that I was grown-up and ready to go back to college.

At Corral de Quati, I found my parents much the same, but my siblings had all moved up in life, and what space I had occupied in the family seemed to have closed up. The little girls were not so little anymore, and they had their own horses. There was one great novelty, but nobody really talked about it: while I was away, they had found oil on the ranch. Some Italian boys I knew came to stay, and I thought they would be interested in the oil wells, so we took the old Chevrolet and drove over to the East Mesa to have a look. When we got back, to my great surprise, my mother took me aside and gave me a fierce dressing-down. I didn't understand at the time, but in her eyes it was as if I had shown them open coffers of bullion.

And in fact, coffers of bullion is exactly what those wells

Sedgwick family on horseback, Christmas vacation, 1950

must have yielded, because the very next year Fuzzy took the oil money plus whatever he was able to get for the house on Long Island, then, keeping Goleta for the time being, he sold Corral de Quati too and bought a ranch called Rancho La-guna de San Francisco that was more than twice as big. It was just on the other side of Los Olivos, only six or seven miles away as the crow flies, so when it came time to move, every-body rode the horses over, but the cattle, all two hundred and fifty of them, had to be transported in trucks. I was away at college at the time of the move, and when I came home, I was taken aback, because literally everything was different. My family had settled into a whole new life. God knows, Cor-ral de Quati had been isolated, but it was part of the regular workaday world, and the new ranch clearly was not. It was Fuzzy's dream, his ideal world, and this was where and how we were going to live from now on. Edie was nine, and it's where and how she lived almost uninterruptedly for the next ten years.

## V

The land starts high up at the foot of Figueroa Mountain and descends in folds and foothills that resolve into high ridges between which valleys begin to form and eventually to flatten until finally the ridges peter out and the valleys join and flow into the larger valley of the Santa Ynez River. The ranch is not on the way anywhere. A small back road ends at the gate, and from there to the barns and the house it's a mile. You follow the curving road, and when you get to the top of the first ridge you begin to see the sweeping valley and the tree-lined creek bed that winds along it between the stubble fields and the next ridge over. The road turns north and starts down, but before you reach the valley floor you come round a bend, and there you can make out the ranch buildings amid a whole lot of trees, and beyond them a low white house that used to be obscured by a centuries-old live oak, but the tree died when Fuzzy did. Before you can really see where you are, though, you have to go all the way to the house and walk right through to the other side; there, straight ahead is Grass Mountain, a low triangular peak that in springtime turns bright orange from all the poppies, and next to it but high above stands Figueroa

Edie and Suky at Laguna, ca. 1952

itself, with the whole mass of hills and ridges rolling down from its foot.

In our day the road crossed a couple of cattle guards, and on its way to the main house it passed between the sheep pens and the weathered wooden cottages of the ranch hands. These stood in a grove of live oak trees, laid out along a couple of short streets, with the foreman's larger house at one side, and at the back of this little settlement, separated from it by a broad dusty area, there was one large barn, with corrals at both sides and more corrals at the back. At right angles to the barn at one side there was a long open shed where the farm machinery was kept, together with a couple of old cars and the bulldozer with which, every year after the rainy season, the foreman, Dee, had to grade the many miles of road that covered the ranch. Not far from the shed stood the henhouses, where the chickens were confined now in cages with wire-netting floors. The point was to allow their droppings to fall through, but because they stood on netting all the time, their feet grew long and twisted, so they couldn't have walked even if someone had let them loose. Hard not to see those henhouses as a metaphor.

The road ended at the main house, where on the left there was a turnaround and a small compound of buildings, all painted white: a garage with its own gas pump and the two bunkhouses from Corral de Quati, which had been moved over here because once again there were not enough bedrooms in the house. At the far side of the garage there was a path leading to the new additions: a tennis court like the one at Goleta, a good-sized pool, and beyond that, my father's capacious studio, which had an apartment for guests attached to it at one side.

The house itself was simple enough, with roofs overhanging brick terraces on the north and south sides. When I entered it the first time, I was expecting the interior to be like Corral de Quati, modest, with unpainted furniture and plain cotton curtains and pictures by Fuzzy and his artist friends on the walls. Instead, it turned out to be luxurious. The floors were carpeted, the curtains were made of rich Fortuny damask, and the bookcases contained sets of books that I hadn't seen since Long Island. The sofas and chairs in the living room were covered in leather, in the dining room there was silver on the table, and I recognized the good furniture and paintings from Goleta. It was clear that everything my parents prized was going to be concentrated here in this place, and efforts had been made to dignify it. Another difference was that the family, which at Corral de Quati had been so dispersed, was now concentrated in very close quarters: the three little girls were inside the house, and the bunkhouses were right outside. Kate's room was beyond the dining room, but Edie and Suky now found themselves down the hall from our parents in a large, sunny bedroom built for the two of them, with their new nurse, Addie, across the way. Quite a change after the years of isolation and independence at Corral de Quati.

I confess I felt completely estranged, homesick for the old ranch and the lovely plundered house in Goleta, but everyone else, including William and Nancy, was excited and happy. However, nobody's happiness compared with my father's. It was gargantuan. Out riding he would pull up his horse and look around, then he would gesture broadly toward the landscape and say, "Just look at this; have you ever seen anything on the face of the earth that is more beautiful?"

Duke was his name, and Laguna was his dukedom. It extended as far as you could see in all directions, and in it our mother was his consort and we children were his progeny; all the rest were either his employees or his guests. He had grown up without money to spare, and now suddenly he was a rich man in his own right and didn't mind if it showed. Pretty soon he bought a pair of sky-blue Mercedes cars, a four-door convertible for my mother and a 190 SL sports car for himself. Then he bought a collection of minor Old Master paintings that had belonged to a Minturn relative, had them restored, and hung them all over the house, works with attributions (some questionable) to artists such as Giovanni Bellini and

Vittore Carpaccio and Gerard David. At the same time, he established a presence in Santa Barbara as the unpaid county planning commissioner; he served on various boards and as the local representative for Harvard, raising money and recruiting students; and he began to develop ambitions to transform the local branch of the University of California into the Harvard of the West. He had always had a lot of vitality, and now he was more exuberant than ever. He seemed to have more of a strut to his walk and a more commanding presence when he entered a room.

The daily routine was the same, except that now Fuzzy did his exercises out by the pool where anybody could see him, glistening with oil and sweat, dressed in nothing but a little white cotton loincloth. It was the evenings that were most different. To my surprise, there were cocktails every night now, so everybody dressed up a bit, and William, who was back in the house again, would appear in a white coat bearing plates of hors d'oeuvres. By the same token, dinner was quite formal and the dishes that Nancy produced were more sophisticated; furthermore, my mother would have wine with dinner, sometimes several glasses, while Fuzzy drank scotch and soda. Afterward there was desultory conversation, no more reading aloud, at least that I ever saw, and anyway at first the little girls had their supper early.

Everybody loved it when there were guests. To us children it meant that the laser beam of our parents' attention was directed elsewhere, and to my father it meant that he had a public. He was a good host, always exuberant and entertaining, and a lively raconteur. At the moment I can only recall a couple of his stories, but you'll get the idea: they tended to be outrageous, and often they cast a glamorous light on him. One was about meeting Prince Yusupof at a dinner party in Paris and hearing him tell the grisly story of murdering Rasputin, how they fed him poison and it had no effect, then they shot him three times, once right in the middle of his forehead, and that failed to kill him, so finally they dragged him down to the river and pushed him through the ice, and even then he kept bobbing back up . . . Another was about the time Fuzzy's uncle Newt called him at Harvard and asked him urgently to come down to Greenwich; he wanted help dislodging Hugo von Hofmannsthal's son Raimund, who had invited himself to stay and showed no signs of leaving. Fuzzy took the train the next morning and arrived in time for lunch, only to find that Raimund had not come down yet. He went up to see, and when he opened the door there was Raimund in bed in black silk pajamas. Fuzzy said, "What's the matter? Is your whole goddam family dead?" and Raimund said, "Yes," and it was true: his brother had committed suicide and his father had died days later of grief. Fuzzy always laughed a lot when he told that story, but that was before his own sons died. And then he had a store of funny anecdotes about his friend Sigourney Chatfield Chatfield-Taylor, who had a cleft palate and a quick wit. He never wore a hat, so one time a lady in a shoe store took him for a clerk and complained that the shoes she was trying on didn't fit. Mr. Chatfield-Taylor said in his muffled cleft-palate voice, which Fuzzy would imitate, "I don't see why you care; your clothes don't either." And when Fuzzy was not telling stories he was always bantering, so the conversation at table was lively when there were guests, and the atmosphere was jolly. As at Goleta, there was a general sense that life was a feast, and to me that was the best thing about my father, that he could create that sense; he had such a huge and joyful appetite for life.

Except during school vacations, the population at Laguna was much smaller than it had been at Corral de Quati. Babbo was back east, Bobby and I were in college, and Pamela and Minty and Jonathan were all in boarding school. So most of the year the little girls were the only children at home. Kate was eleven now and growing up, and the new nurse, Addie, cared mainly for Edie and Suky. Addie was the dearest, kindest person you ever saw, although far too gentle to deal with a child like Edie. I had always assumed that Addie came because Sophie retired, but just the other day Jonathan told me what really happened: Edie got Sophie fired. I couldn't believe it. Most of us children had been spanked all our lives, and we were used to it. Fuzzy would smack us with a hairbrush, but Sophie used one of her springy shoe trees, the kind with a wooden toe and heel and a steel band in between, and it really stung. It seems that one day in the cottage at Corral de Quati Edie did something naughty and Sophie spanked her for it. Edie ran straight to Mummy and Fuzzy and complained and carried on until next thing you know, they fired Sophie— Sophie, who had been with us most of our lives, ever since Long Island! I have no idea where the poor woman went or what became of her. Edie couldn't have been more than seven or eight years old at the time.

At Laguna, Edie and Suky became inseparable, and now, within the larger world that our parents were creating there, Edie created an ideal world for the two of them. Curiously, there was no mother in the family she invented, just an

76

Indian chief and a whole bunch of children, and the father was kind and never punished anybody. Suky said how happy they were in that imaginary world. Suky had started on the piano by then, and Edie drew all the time, mainly horses. She also made elaborate stick horses for the two of them, and you would come upon them in the driveway or out on the lawn, whinnying and snorting and prancing about. So now Fuzzy noticed them, and he began calling them Miss Rembrandt and Miss Mozart and showing them off to visitors. At the same time, my mother drew them close to her, and the pleasure she took in them makes me wonder now whose idea it had been to move them out of the house at Corral de Quati. She brought them to Cambridge for a visit one time when they were eight and ten, and I remember being shocked to see how babyish they were. They called her "Mum-Mum" and clung to her, holding tight to her hands, whereas when I was ten I was away at school and felt pretty grown-up.

I cannot honestly say I knew my little sisters in those years, because I came home less and less. In fact, after the move to Laguna, I wasn't close to anybody, because at that time they all belonged to the hermetic world of the ranch, where one had to enjoy the approval of our parents in order to belong, and I never did. I was back at college, zigging and zagging along, but far more successfully than before (although it turned out Fuzzy didn't think so). Whenever I did go to the ranch, it was vacation, and not only was everyone else home, but there were always masses of other people around, incidental visitors who arrived for lunch and others who were staying: old family friends from the East, schoolmates of Bobby's and Pamela's, Kate's best friend, all playing tennis or fooling around by the pool, laughing and joking. Everybody always seemed to be having a wonderful time. Fuzzy was at the center of it all, always, more boisterous than ever, teasing and flirting and peacocking about, but he and my mother seemed comfortable together. A beautiful, ideal family leading a beautiful, ideal life was the image. Everyone who visited the ranch was dazzled by it. Even I was dazzled, and I would have given anything to be part of it. To be honest, the only time I felt at home was when I was on a horse, working cattle, but then I was in heaven. The afternoons were hot and sunny, the sky was cloudless, and there I was, out hooting and hollering and moving cows along ahead of me. More than anything, I loved to ride alone in that immense and exhilarating landscape. There are no words to express the feeling—only music, only a Brahms symphony, comes close.

All three little girls were like centaurs. They rode bareback with tie ropes looped round their horses' noses, and even for cattle work in steep country I rarely saw them use saddles, just pads strapped on with surcingles. Edie particularly loved to ride at night. She and Suky would go galloping flat out in the stubble fields, and I know why. Riding in darkness under the moon and stars is like floating; it's like riding in the waves, because you can't really see the ground, you can only feel, and the feeling is pure exaltation. Edie also found it exhilarating to ride in a storm. At Corral de Quati, the violence of nature had never made itself felt, but at Goleta it certainly had. I remember as a very small child waking up and seeing the entire mountain range behind the house in flames, and sometimes the house would shake and rattle as the earth moved beneath it. Even the tumultuous roar of the wind in the eucalyptus at

**Edie on Rumpelstiltskin, ca. 1957**

night was enough to carry me into a state bordering on existential dread. Here at Laguna, Edie and Suky had a view from their windows right across the valley to the coastal range, so they could see the huge exploding fires that lit up the sky in summer, and in winter they could watch the storms. And now that they could ride anywhere on their own, they were out in the landscape experiencing it all. As Suky described it, "We *lived* the seasons! It was living in an absolute. If you have the galaxies above you and the changing seasons below you, you live in another dimension, and the only thing we had beside that were a few skimpy little actors on our stage, and that's all." That will tell you the sense of scale that Edie grew up with. It also suggests how she might have arrived at her ideas about the cosmos and space and the situation of the human race, all those ideas that she was so eager to communicate once she got out into the world. What Edie wanted, always, was to experience life with the greatest intensity, and she had no regard for danger. It's risky to ride in a storm because of lightning, and it's risky to gallop like that in the dark, because your horse could spook or step in a hole, but Edie was completely fearless and always did what she wanted. By the same token she also got what she wanted, and the boys in particular would be angry when they came home for vacation to find that she had persuaded our parents to let her have somebody's favorite horse. Whatever it was, whatever it cost, whomever it belonged to, if Edie coveted it she got it. Another thing, if she wanted something and Fuzzy said no, my mother would invariably give in to her, and once or twice, for the first time ever, I saw my parents disagree angrily. On the other hand, I never saw either one of them discipline Edie, and that was galling, given all the criticism and shaming some of us had been subjected to.

It turned out that these were not the only tensions on the ranch, under the mythic surface, because Bobby had begun having anxiety attacks (it started at school, and Mummy came

east to deal with it; she said it was due to a chemical imbal-
ance in his brain) and Minty was drinking too much. Perhaps
that's why my parents suddenly cracked down on me—maybe
the explanation is that they were alarmed and took it out
on me, because what they did was this: they stopped paying
my tuition bills, and Fuzzy came east, went to the dean, and
said all kinds of terrible things to get me kicked out. Then
he came to me and demanded that I transfer to a women's
college on the West Coast. When I refused, he said I had to
go into the army. We had a horrendous fight at my grandmother's house on Long Island, after which Fuzzy took me
to a dinner party with friends of his. On the way he said such
awful things that I sat silent and weepy through most of the
evening, and when we got home I went straight to my room.
I was sitting on my bed, still in my evening dress, when Fuzzy
came in, sat down next to me, and put his arms around me.
Then he put his head on my bare shoulder and said he could
understand how men felt about me; he was a man himself. It
stopped there, but that was enough. I thought, *So* that's *what
this has all been about?* and for the first time I felt contempt
for my father.

I mention this because when Edie got to New York she told
everybody she had been subjected to Fuzzy's sexual advances
from the age of seven. Now, that's impossible, because when
Edie was seven she lived in the cottage at Corral de Quati with
Sophie and the others, and according to Kate, they hardly ever
saw him. But when Edie found she had an audience, she told
so many tall tales about Fuzzy that people thought she was

obsessed with him. For instance, she told Isabel Eberstadt that he had once made Suky and her take off their shirts and sit, bare-breasted like two sphinxes, on columns at either side of the gate to the ranch, and that he would beat them brutally if they so much as moved. That's completely absurd, but when it comes to sexual advances, all I know is what Edie claimed, and the fact that I find it hard to believe doesn't mean some of it couldn't have been true.

Fortunately for me, I was able to show the dean a letter from my mother saying they had paid the tuition when in fact they had not. I don't know what the dean made of my father's behavior, but I was allowed to stay on. A friend lent me the money for summer school, but after that I couldn't pay, so I withdrew, planning to earn some money and go back as soon as I was solvent. Meanwhile, I cut myself off from my family.

## VI

A year or two passed. On the ranch, life went on and the surface continued to hold, and now Pamela got engaged. What's more, to the great surprise of my family, so did I, and it looked as if I too had managed to follow my parents' way. I had moved to Georgetown, where I shared a house with a friend of a friend and worked in a bookstore while looking around for something better. One evening I was sitting on the sofa reading *The Tempest* aloud with a guy I knew (this was the fifties, when single girls with no money could live on N Street, and when some people's idea of a date was reading *The Tempest*) and my roommate came laughing through the door with a very tall, very handsome young man in a tan gabardine suit. I had never seen him before, even though it turned out we had been in the same year at college. She introduced him as her cousin, on leave from the army; we talked a bit, and the next day he invited me to dinner. He turned out to represent every single thing I had been taught that a man was supposed to be and do—not only had he been senior prefect at Groton and president of the Porcellian, but he had also graduated with honors in math and rowed on a legendary crew—and on top of it all he was a modest and honorable person. I was lost in admiration; however, I recognized, and was touched to understand, that with all that perfection he had not had much experience of life. As for me, I might have seemed sophisticated, but I was still really clueless, and except for that one affair in college I had never had a real relationship either. We were both twenty-two. I thought I was really old to be getting married, and I suspect he feared that he was really young, but in those days you just assumed that once you got on the conveyor belt of marriage it would carry you through all of life's successive stages.

Pamela's wedding was set for August 14, 1954, her nineteenth birthday, and mine was to be a few weeks later. I arrived at the airport in Santa Barbara the day before her bridal dinner, and I wasn't feeling well; it turned out I had a fever of 104. Meanwhile, that same afternoon, on the other side of town, a car crowded my brother Bobby off the road on his bike, and he broke his neck. We didn't know it then, but that was the beginning of the years of wreckage. Bobby was taken to Cottage

Hospital, where he spent the night in traction, awaiting the operation that would save him from paralysis. I was put in isolation at Goleta, in the guesthouse, along with a nervous young German shepherd my parents had just been given. First thing the next morning, I called my brother to wish him luck, and he told me he had had a nightmare. He'd dreamt that he crawled on his knees down the little corridor that led to our parents' bedroom door and begged them to give him another chance; he begged and begged, and they told him no, that he had used up all his chances.

But that was behind the scenes. On the main stage, I was told, the bridal dinner went off beautifully; so did the wedding the next afternoon, and a few days later Pamela and her new husband headed for New York in the canary-yellow convertible our parents had given them as a wedding present. Offstage, Bobby's neck was successfully fused, and after a week or two he was taken home to the ranch in a huge carapace of white plaster with a cage at the top for his head, which was fixed to it by four rods embedded in his skull. All I had was a bad case of mononucleosis, but apparently it was contagious, so Grandma took me to stay with her in a very nice hotel in Santa Barbara until the doctor said I could go home. It was October and I had turned twenty-three before I was well enough to be married.

My husband was based at Fort Holabird in Baltimore, so we spent the winter in a farmhouse in hunting country, and after he got out of the army, we moved to Cambridge for graduate school. Pamela was already there with her husband, who was beginning his postponed senior year, and she was expecting a baby. She had just turned twenty. Bobby was there too, back in Eliot House, trying to finish his degree and seeing a psychiatrist for his anxiety attacks and mood swings, and meanwhile he and Peter Sourian had an exotic waif called Gregory Corso living secretly in a tent in their room. You cannot imagine what a sensation Gregory created in Cambridge. He was a street kid still, just out of Dannemora, the maximum-security prison where he had done three years for robbery, and while he was there an old guy had introduced him to reading. He had read everything you can think of, from Stendhal and the Russians to Joyce, plus the complete works of Will and Ariel Durant, and his idol was the poet Shelley. Somehow he had found his way to Harvard, and here he was, writing poetry and living from hand to mouth among the privileged, who couldn't get enough of him. So some fissures had opened up in my brother's life. He had turned away from our parents and the Porcellian Club and was reading about philosophy and Zen Buddhism. At some point he acquired an old black Porsche, and with his brooding good looks he cut quite a figure around Cambridge. I took him very seriously—he made me think of Stavrogin in *The Possessed*—and so did some of his teachers; others, however, were put off by his extreme ideas and erratic behavior. Of course I knew he was having difficulties and that they were painful, but at that point I had complete faith in psychiatry and all the new drugs that were coming out, and it never once crossed my mind that my brother was not going to be just fine. That's how clueless I was. He got his degree and enrolled in graduate school to study Oriental art (as they called it then), so for the next few years we saw each other pretty constantly, and it was during that time that he became a doctrinaire Marxist. I didn't know it until long afterward, but improbably enough it was Morty Sills, the proprietor of the gentlemen's clothing store on Mount Auburn Street, whose name is now a trademark, who introduced him into the Communist Party. And then Bobby just vanished. It turned out he had taken off for Kansas City to work as an organizer for the ILGWU, and what with one thing and another, including a lot of suffering, he did not get back to Cambridge and graduate school until the spring of 1964, by which time I was long gone and Edie was there.

So Bobby was not around in February 1957, when that Groton letter came out, but my husband received it, and so did various Sedgwick cousins and a number of people we knew. For weeks everybody was talking about it and speculating as to who could have done such a thing. And then, as I said, my cousin Alexander Sedgwick came and told me. I was stunned and ashamed when I learned that it was my father, the descendant of generations of dedicated abolitionists on both sides, *my father*, who had written that letter, but at the same time I was relieved. I thought, *My God, he's crazy—this means he is really crazy, and now it's clear for anybody to see.* Until that moment there had been no overt evidence of my father's dark side, and we children, who bore the brunt of it, had been taught from infancy to respect and admire him. I was sure this would be it, the end of his perfect public image, but in the event the school did not press charges, and the whole thing seemed to blow over. (Fuzzy himself was unfazed: after Minty died he sent out another letter to everyone associated with

Groton School, in which he blamed the school and its head-master for Minty's suicide, and this time he signed it.)

I had always known people in Cambridge who were involved in radical politics, but at that stage and for a long time after-ward, nobody I knew had anything to do with drugs. Then one day a friend who was getting a degree in psychology in-vited me to sit in on a program at Boston Psychopathic Hos-pital that was experimenting with a drug called lysergic acid diethylamide. He explained that it induced a state resem-bling schizophrenia, and they wanted to see if it was useful in treating mental illness. So for some weeks I watched as small groups of volunteers—all men, all medical or doctoral stu-dents from Harvard—sat around in a circle and did or did not react to randomly administered injections of LSD, grain alco-hol, or just plain water. I personally never saw anyone develop the full-blown symptoms of schizophrenia, but I heard a hor-ror story about a medical student who escaped in a psychotic state and ran all over town for days on end, and I did see a number of guys break down. Interestingly, it was usually the straightest guys, the all-American ones who looked the most confident and self-possessed, who would wind up sobbing and saying they had never lived up to somebody or other's ex-pectations, while the nerdy, neurotic ones just went on acting nerdy and neurotic. Eventually, I was assigned to a program that was investigating the use of drugs in mental hospitals to control violent patients, and I went to work as a volunteer in the locked wards at Waltham State. Then one day my cousin

Johnny Marquand, who had heard what I was up to, called from New York and asked if he could bring a friend to stay. The friend turned out to be a rangy Scot by the name of Alex Trocchi, who knew so much about LSD and about drug-testing programs around the country that I assumed he was a doctor, but no, he was a writer, a very famous writer of pornography, he said, and he was living on a garbage scow on the Hudson. What he wanted was access to LSD. However, this was before the days of Timothy Leary and Richard Alpert, and the program at Boston Psychopathic was closed to outsiders. Decades passed before I learned that the experiments I had witnessed were part of MK-ULTRA, the secret program that the CIA had set up at Harvard in 1952, the real object of which was to study how drugs could be used to control human minds, or in other words, for brainwashing.

Not long after that, my marriage came apart. We were not grown-up enough to deal with our difficulties; it turned out we had been playing house all along, living "as if." So in the fall of 1958 I moved to New York and through friends I got a job at a settlement house in East Harlem working with Black and Hispanic kids. Areas were being razed all around, housing projects were going up, drugs—mainly heroin—were infiltrating everywhere, and the tension between the two communities was fierce. I found that out on the first day when an eight-year-old boy asked me for a black crayon so he could draw a picture of Eddie's mother. Eddie shot out of the room, and next thing I knew, back he came with his father, who was carrying a knife. And then, within seconds, my supervisor appeared and took care of the situation. Agnes Preston was her name; she was a tiny elegant Black lady in her forties with a bunch of advanced degrees, and there she got an angry young guy to back up and put away his knife. Then she called me into her office and told me some basic things I needed to know about the situation between the two communities. It was the first of innumerable lessons I learned from her. I had had absolutely no notion of the Hispanic presence in New York, and up to then I had encountered very few people of color. In Cambridge I had been aware of Jane Bunche, the president of my class, whose father was undersecretary of the UN, and Lena Horne's daughter, Gail Jones, and I had known a remarkable girl called Dorothy Dean. Dorothy and I had been students together in the fine arts department, and she was so clever and sharp-tongued, and always kept such clever company, that to me she was just another super-smart Radcliffe girl. Bobby had been talking a lot about slavery and the situation of the Blacks ("Negroes," we still said) in American society, but he always spoke in abstract terms of capitalist exploitation and class struggle, and I don't know if at that point he knew anyone who was directly involved (although he did have friends later on who went to Selma). Here in East Harlem, the situation was on everyone's mind, and the atmosphere was electric, not least because Malcolm X was speaking and holding meetings blocks away. Agnes Preston was going with a colleague, and there was a lot of discussion among the staff. I wanted to go too but was told I would not be welcome, which was an important lesson right there. I would go out to dinner with Agnes and her friend, and they had to pick the restaurant, because in midtown Manhattan in the 1950s there were very few places that would serve them, and that was another lesson: I had had no idea that their map of the city was so different from mine. They talked about the drug situation (Agnes Preston's view was that the Mafia was deliberately anesthetizing the Black community to keep things quiet around their operations), and they argued a lot about Malcolm. They would pit his vision against what Martin Luther King was preaching in the South, and both of them came down on the side of Malcolm. Then when I ventured to ask about James Baldwin, whom I admired, I was surprised to hear that neither Agnes nor her friend took him seriously at all. In fact, Agnes made wicked fun of him (more lessons). You have to remember, at that point *Brown v. Board of Education* was only a couple of years old, and down in Montgomery the boycott was in progress. All the rest was to come, and the world around me felt pregnant with it.

Edie, meanwhile, had gone off to boarding school at Branson's in the fall of '56. She was only thirteen and had never been off the ranch, never been anywhere on her own. Although she had always dominated whatever situation she encountered, when she went away to school she couldn't manage, and by spring she was back at home. I heard she had a serious disease—somebody said it was leukemia, but clearly that was not the case. My guess is that already at that stage it was bulimia, but it could simply have been severe homesickness, or perhaps it was a combination.

Whatever it was, for the next year and a half she was kept at home on the ranch; only Suky was there. Everyone else was away at school. When they came home for Christmas in 1957, Edie was not to be seen, and they were told she was sick. All they knew was that she was being kept in bed, and every few days the doctor came and sedated her. It was years before they heard Edie's side of the story; then what she told them was this:

Edie said she walked into the blue sitting room one day, and there was Fuzzy on the floor like a dog, mounting a beautiful young wife we all knew. She ran out of the room crying, Fuzzy followed her and smacked her, then he called the doctor and said she was crazy; the doctor came and put her to bed and shot her full of tranquilizers; Edie told Mummy what she had seen, Mummy wouldn't believe her, no one would believe her, and after that she was kept in a darkened room, half-drugged all the time.

When I first heard this story I couldn't see how it was possible. To begin with, the doctor might have believed my father, but why would Mummy have refused to believe Edie? She knew Fuzzy was unfaithful; she had been covering for him for years. He didn't even conceal it from her when that beautiful young wife or another needed an abortion. (I know because Fuzzy wrote to his psychiatrist telling him all about it, and years later I saw the letter with my own eyes.) How then is it conceivable that she could look her favorite, most beloved child in the eye and say she didn't believe her?

Ah, but on the ranch the line was that Edie was mentally ill, so there was no reason to believe a word she said.

Edie's story means that on the ranch the truth was whatever our father and mother said it was. It means they could and did compel their children to live as if it were so. It also means that our mother's sole enterprise in life was to sustain her husband and their common understanding at whatever cost to herself or her children, even Edie.

———

When Suky went away to Branson's in the fall of 1958, our parents must have thought Edie was well enough to try again, because they sent her east to St. Timothy's. She was following in the footsteps of both Pamela, who had done really well there, and Kate, who had been so unhappy that she left after a year and went to study in Florence. For Edie, everything began auspiciously—she was wildly popular, the absolute center of attention in the entire school, and she was voted president of her class—but after creating such an extraordinary vortex around herself she couldn't keep it up. She began having tantrums and breaking rules, and while she may have made it through the year, she didn't go back. From then on she stayed on the ranch, where most of the time she was alone with our parents.

I knew nothing of all this in the summer of 1960, when I went home for the first time in six years. Bobby was in the East and Minty and Jonathan were in the army, but everyone else was there when I arrived. Pamela had come down from San Francisco with her family, and I found her over by the pool attending to a baby girl. Her two little boys were splashing about, clamoring for her to watch, and her husband was just coming off the tennis court, bright red in the face from the heat after losing to Fuzzy (who played a mean-spirited game, always fanning and cutting the ball to get a spin on it). Kate was also there by the pool, talking to a friend; she was tall and slender now, and her curly hair was cut very short. I didn't see Edie or Suky until lunchtime. I remember it distinctly. I was standing in the dining room when they came wandering in and suddenly saw me. Both of them stopped and stared, as if I were a complete foreigner, and I myself felt equally estranged, because those shy little girls were teenagers now, and taller than I was. They were nice-looking, both of them, but a bit unformed, and it was not clear that they were going to be all that beautiful. However, looks were on Edie's mind: one day she asked me outright if I didn't think she was the most beautiful girl in the family, with the best legs. She was seventeen years old and I was nearly thirty, and here she was demanding that I acknowledge her preeminence. And she *was* preeminent. It looked to me as if she had completely subjugated my mother and father, and she had her way with everybody and everything on the ranch.

The signs of Edie's dominance were everywhere. She had Addie's old room, and to my astonishment all the good English furniture had been removed and replaced with truly hideous heart-shaped pieces designed by Edie herself. It must have cost a fortune to have them made. What on earth had come over my parents, that they went along with that? She also had a gorgeous new saddle, specially built and hand-tooled, which she hardly used, and she had been given Jonathan's very handsome horse. On top of it all, she had a horrid white rat for a pet. And then there were her eating habits. At every meal she would take enormous helpings, wolf it all down, and disappear; after a few minutes she would return and begin all over again. I had never seen that before and I didn't know the name for it, although at boarding school I had heard that if you didn't want to get fat you could put your finger down your throat and make yourself throw up. I had also heard that it could kill you if you got in the habit. Nobody said a word, though, and that was typical. In our family nobody ever said a word about what was going on under the surface. Appearances were everything, and we lived by them.

At the same time, my mother was having special food prepared for her, and I was told she had developed a whole lot of new allergies. Moreover, to my surprise, she was drinking straight whiskey, a couple of tumblers, before dinner. I got the impression Fuzzy was plying her with it. Both my parents had always taken quantities of pills (even when we lived in the farmhouse at Nethermuir, I remember they each had an array laid out before them on the breakfast table, and they were only in their twenties then), and now my mother was taking a lot more, including tranquilizers, which was something new. My father for his part was taking what he called his "bennies" for asthma, which probably contributed to his unregulated behavior. Publicly, he had become an important patron: he was negotiating with UC Santa Barbara to leave the ranch to them, and everybody in the county knew about it. It was to be the largest gift the university had ever received up to that point, and not only that, he was planning to give them his collection of paintings to found a museum in his name. My mother remained in the background, and I thought she seemed somehow harder. For the first time I heard her swear. As for the daily routine, it was the same as always, except that now not everyone rode. I don't remember that Edie ever came riding while I was there, but I do remember a couple of times waiting for her to appear and my parents arguing disagreeably about whether she should be made to come.

One evening they gave one of their big parties in the studio, with tables indoors and out, masses of food, and more liquor than I had ever seen on the ranch. The image I have in my memory looks like a Fellini film set in Southern California. There were old friends, mostly transplanted easterners and sunburnt ranchers and their wives, and a whole lot of new people: hearty middle-aged men, loud talkers, women in bright dresses, and handsome couples in their thirties. At Goleta, Fuzzy had always said they gave two kinds of parties, vertical in the house and horizontal in the studio, and this party at Laguna was both. People would drift outside, talking desultorily with drinks in their hands, and some would wander in pairs into the darkness. I was sitting indoors at a table with a youngish couple, a violinist and his wife who appeared to be very close to my parents, and as we were talking I saw my father get up from his table, put his arm around a blowsy middle-aged woman who laughed a lot, and walk out the door right in front of my mother and everybody else.

I don't remember seeing Edie or Suky that evening, but they did appear another time, when we were all invited to a party at the Perkinses' ranch in Happy Canyon. Everybody was dressed and ready to go, and we were just waiting for Edie. After a while, Mummy went to see while the rest of us waited and waited, and then it was as if a Hollywood starlet were emerging onto a runway. Edie was all made-up, and she had on a fancy dress with a tight waist and a bouffant skirt. She carried herself, and Mummy attended her, as if all eyes were upon her as she went out the front door.

After that summer of 1960 it was a while before I went back to the ranch, but I kept hearing from my siblings that Edie was getting more and more out of control. Then I heard that my parents had decided to take her to Vienna. The idea was that she would live there for a year with an aristocratic family they knew.

## VII

It was the fall of 1962; Edie was nineteen. And meanwhile, in January of that year, my real life had suddenly commenced. A friend who played the violin called and said he had invited another violinist, a German art historian from Yale, and would I come and accompany them on the harpsichord. I had played chamber music with amateur groups in Cambridge, and the other participants were often middle-aged refugees from Austria and Germany, so that's what I was expecting. Instead, in walked somebody who looked more like a ski instructor. The three of us played for a while, and when our host went to the kitchen to see about supper, the professor suggested that he and I play a Mozart sonata. (He was a far more accomplished musician than I was, but he always said that after the first movement he knew me by the way I played.) Then we talked and it turned out that music was not all that we had in common, so to make a long story short, pretty soon we moved in together, and on November 20, 1962, we went down to city hall and got married.

I had seen Edie earlier that fall at my grandmother's apartment at 720 Park Avenue. Our parents had taken her to Vienna all right, but my mother and Edie had come straight back. It seems that the night they got there the three of them had gone down to dinner in the hotel, and I don't know whether it was that he hadn't noticed, or that he was seeing her for the first time away from the ranch, or what it was, but when Fuzzy saw that Edie couldn't control herself, that she was wolfing her food and leaving the table and coming back and beginning all over again, he suddenly put his foot down and said this couldn't go on, she had to be hospitalized *now*. It seems my mother resisted, and oh my God, what a fight that must have been. Apparently, there were threats of divorce, and when they parted the next day it was not at all clear what my mother would do. Fuzzy flew to London to meet Jonathan, who was coming in from Germany on leave from the army, and Jonathan says when he got there he found Fuzzy in a shocking state; he looked as if he was on the edge of a breakdown, and he was sure Mummy had left him. According to Jonathan, the whole week they were in London, Fuzzy was just praying that she would do as he said and put Edie in the hospital. And indeed, when I got to Grandma's that day, that's exactly what Mummy was doing. She was in the library with the sliding doors closed, making arrangements for Edie to go to Silver Hill in New Canaan, Connecticut. That's when, for the first and only time that I can remember, I heard my mother cry. Finally, when she came out she told me Fuzzy had threatened to leave if she didn't put Edie in the hospital, and I said that meant she had to choose between her husband and her children. She said there was no question of leaving her husband—she couldn't. And as for Edie herself, who was at the center of it all, she seemed perfectly composed. She was all dolled up, with a beehive hairdo and a ton of makeup, and at lunch she stuffed herself, left the table, and came back to begin all over again, acting the whole time as if what was taking place had nothing to do with her.

My parents knew about Silver Hill because it was founded by Dr. John Millet, the psychiatrist who had treated Fuzzy at the Austen Riggs Center in Stockbridge before they were married. (By the way, it was Dr. Millet who warned them that they should not have children, and they went ahead anyway and had eight. Anything to prove that there was nothing wrong with my father.) Fuzzy had stayed in close touch with him, always painting a rosy picture of our family life to show the doctor how wrong he had been. At a certain point, however, he began asking for advice about Minty, complaining that he was not manly, that he was refusing to play football at Groton, that he was fearful, and so forth. And in fact, poor Minty was so terrified of flying that one time on his way back to school he hid in the men's room in the LA airport until after the plane took off. But then, diffident and gentle as he was, he did surprisingly well in the army. He had always been a good shot, and now he got a medal for it in basic training and spent three good years at the Monterey School of Languages studying Mandarin Chinese; when he left, they gave him their highest rating and all kinds of commendations. Too bad Minty didn't stay in the army, where the structure might have sustained him, because when he got out, he couldn't handle Harvard. He was completely overwhelmed and his drinking got out of control. In the fall of 1961, he took a leave of absence and came to live in New York, in a borrowed apartment on the Upper East Side. I kept in close touch, trying to help, and one morning I got a bizarre call from him. When I got over there he came to the door in his pajamas, all spattered with blood, holding a little metal baton in his hand, and behind him, I remember, the phonograph was blasting out the Spring Symphony. I took him to Payne Whitney and persuaded him to commit himself, and after a week or two my parents had him transferred to Silver Hill. He did well there—or so it seemed. When he got out he joined AA and went regularly to meetings, and he enrolled in the School of General Studies at Columbia. So my mother must have had high hopes when she took Edie to Silver Hill.

But that place was no match for Edie. She held her head high and took the attitude that there was nothing the matter with her, that Fuzzy was simply trying to get rid of her. In her mind it must have been a repetition of the time on the ranch when he called the doctor and had her drugged and made everybody believe she was crazy. She even seemed to be enjoying herself whenever I visited. She had friends, and to my eye the place looked more like a nice country hotel than a hospital. Also, she was free to come and go, so she was spending a shocking amount of money shopping in New Canaan. She never mentioned her doctor or whatever treatment she was getting, but I could see that she liked the occupational therapy, because she showed me some exquisite drawings that she had made of mice and other small creatures, as well as some useful objects in wood and clay. However, she kept on stuffing herself and vomiting and stuffing and vomiting until finally she got down to less than a hundred pounds and stopped menstruating. That was more than Silver Hill could handle, so she was moved to a closed hospital in White Plains, called Bloomingdale.

It turned out to be the modern incarnation of the old Bloomingdale Insane Asylum, and although it stood on a high hill amid handsomely landscaped grounds, it was no country inn. They put Edie straight into a closed ward under the care of a terrific no-nonsense doctor named Jane O'Neill, and both the doctor and the regimen were extremely strict. Edie was kept under constant observation, her diet was carefully monitored, and at the beginning, to my dismay, she was subjected to a course of shock treatments. As you might imagine, she hated it. She couldn't stand the confinement and all the restrictions, but once she understood that there was no way round the program, she figured it out. She began cooperating like a little angel and doing everything in her power to get out. I know, because I visited her every week unless my mother was in town, and I could see how well she was doing. I watched her graduate steadily from ward to ward, earning more freedom and responsibility at every stage (although at the same time, she would boast to me about breaking rules and getting away with it). Still, I could see a change every time I went, until she seemed like a different person entirely. She stopped teasing her hair, stopped using makeup, and became truly beautiful, just a pure, natural beauty. I thought I was seeing her genuine self at last. I really thought she had learned how to take charge of her life, but now I think what I was seeing was a creature in a trap, fighting with everything she had to get free. She seemed so innocent and childlike that I was stricken with pity for her and would sometimes find myself driving away in tears.

Edie was still at Bloomingdale late that spring when to my surprise and joy I found out I was going to have a baby. When summer came, my husband and I went away to Nantucket to get out of the heat, and by the time we got home Edie was back at the ranch, and it was a long time before I saw her again. Meanwhile, I learned that she too had gotten pregnant that spring. I was told it happened at Grandma's, when she was on leave from Bloomingdale at the end of her time there, and she was supposed to be demonstrating how responsible she was. I believe it was her first experience of sex. However, she had no difficulty getting an abortion, and the whole episode didn't appear to have made any difference, since the hospital discharged her shortly afterward. She went home and spent the rest of the summer on the ranch. Nobody around her out there would have been paying attention to what was going on in the world, so I am sure Edie never heard about the March on Washington that took place at the end of August, and I am equally sure my parents didn't tell her when I called them about Bobby.

This was the season of wreckage. Bobby had walked away from his job in Kansas City and was back in New York, living aimlessly in a railroad apartment on the Lower East Side. It was clear that he had lost his bearings, so when he called me on August 20 sounding disoriented, I was alarmed but not completely unprepared. I told him to get in a cab, and while I waited for him to arrive I called the ranch and asked my parents for help. I begged and begged, getting more and more frantic as they equivocated, until Fuzzy said I was upsetting my mother and hung up on me. My husband and I didn't have the money for a private hospital, so I called Edie's doctor at Bloomingdale, and she told me to calm down and take my brother to Bellevue. She said it was fine for him to go there to be evaluated. So that's what I had to do: I had to take him to Bellevue and leave him there. A day or two later, they sent him over to Manhattan State Hospital, that hulking place on Wards Island under the Triborough Bridge, where we visited him until at last my parents came through and arranged for him to be moved to the Hartford Retreat in Connecticut. That's where he was in January, when my baby was born, and he was still there in March, when Minty died. I have no idea how he found out.

Edie spent that summer just waiting to leave home and live on her own. She was twenty years old, and unless you count those brief stints in boarding schools and mental hospitals she had no experience whatever of the world beyond the ranch. She had no education to speak of, no idea how to take care of herself or do the least thing of a practical nature, and of course, no sense whatever of limits. But Edie didn't know ⋅ the difference, and as it turned out, all that was just part of her magic. She had her looks and her captivating manner, she had that great steamrolling way about her, and she couldn't wait to see what life might hold for her once she was free and on her own. When September came round, my mother took her east and settled her in Cambridge to study sculpture with Fuzzy's cousin Lily Saarinen.

# VIII

The plan was a success, at least for a time. Cousin Lily was a fine sculptor, and she was absolutely crazy about Edie. She always said Edie was the most talented student she ever had; she wound up devoting all her time to her, and she forgave her when she brought crowds of friends along to her lessons and began showing up more and more erratically. So far as I know, the only sculpture Edie ever made was a clay figure of a horse, and she never finished it. I kept hearing about it, and I expected it to be either romantic like her drawings or realistic like the statue that Fuzzy was working on at the time. So when I saw a photograph I got a shock. Not that it wasn't handsome, but Edie's famous sculpture looked like a cross between a cart horse and the T'ang sculpture that Mummy had made into a lamp after Fuzzy pronounced it a fake. To judge from the pictures, the horse was no more than eighteen inches tall, but it was massive and its feet were set foursquare in a frame, so it appeared to be immobilized. Only the head suggested movement: it was raised unnaturally high, as if to trumpet a longing for freedom. Edie fussed over that thing for most of the year, and pretty soon everybody in Cambridge knew about it.

Right from the start, Edie was conspicuous. She appeared on the scene as if from nowhere, beautiful, unattached, and eager for life. She was also unimaginably innocent, because literally everything was new to her. She had no experience, no frame of reference, no sense of scale, and no standards by which to calibrate her behavior or evaluate what she encountered. She was open and alive to absolutely everything, and that, together with her beauty and her enchanting presence, made her irresistible.

At first her life was exactly what our parents had in mind. Jonathan was out of the army and back at Harvard, so she went to his parties and met his friends, many of whom belonged to the Porcellian. Suky was also in Cambridge, studying the piano, although she told me they didn't see much of each other, only when Edie was upset. Both girls went to the coming-out parties that fall, and Edie met more people that way. Meanwhile, Jonathan introduced her to the Casablanca, the famous bar at the Brattle Theater, which had a certain atmosphere, and right away she made it her headquarters, even though for most of that year she wasn't old enough to drink and had no business being there. So one way and another Edie met more and more people, and soon she had a very attractive beau called Bartle Bull, with whom she went everywhere. At this point there was a certain rhythm to her life: during the day she saw her psychiatrist and went to her sculpture lessons, driving herself about in a big gray Mercedes sedan, and every night she was out.

Edie's new life was like those Japanese clamshells that you drop into a glass of water. At first it was closed, but now it began to open, and a gaudy flower appeared and floated toward the surface. Somewhere she encountered a lighthearted Harvard senior called Ed Hennessy, who was known for his droll turns of phrase and travesti impersonations of Bea Lillie. And then, through Ed, she met a smooth young dandy from Pittsburgh called Chuck Wein. Now, Ed Hennessy was wonderful company, carefree and cozy, but Chuck Wein was something else. He had graduated from Harvard the year before with a sophisticated thesis on Pirandello's *Six Characters in Search of an Author*, and since then he had been traveling the world in pursuit of his interests, which were said to be esoteric; most recently, he had been living in Tangiers and tutoring the son of William Burroughs. So he got around. Now he was back in Cambridge, keeping himself afloat by playing the horses. Chuck took to Edie on sight, and he and Ed became her constant companions. They accompanied her, she accompanied them, and it was with them that she entered the world of alternative conventions.

The gay netherworld had existed forever on the fringes of Harvard; I myself had glimpsed it when I was there. It was populated mainly by graduate school dropouts lingering on in Cambridge, quaintly mannered Bostonians and languid Southerners living on their inheritances, and the eccentric women who frequented them. Now, in the early sixties, it revolved around a brilliant onetime graduate student who went by the name of Ed Hood or the alias Cloke Dosset. He was a sleek, roundish Southerner, from Alabama, I think it was, with a seriously bad reputation—he was said to be so predatory with undergraduates that he was banned from entering Harvard Yard. His tiny apartment across from the back door of the Casablanca was a late-night destination, and his bed was widely known as Logan Airport. The whole milieu was unlike anything in Edie's experience—lively, sophisticated, and wildly free; it was also outlandish, louche, and a lot of fun— and she really took to it. She was never altogether comfortable with straight men and would complain of their attention while at the same time doing everything possible to attract it. The truth is, she was not looking for sex or marriage, and although she would readily engage in intense conversation, it was not even relationships that she was after. What she craved was to be out in the world experiencing life; she wanted excitement, fun, and a public, so the gay guys suited her perfectly, and she suited them. They adored her. Through Ed Hennessy and Chuck, she got to know Ed Hood, and through him she met a classicist called Donald Lyons and a law student by the name of Gordon Baldwin; then through Chuck she met a footloose undergraduate named Tommy Goodwin, who was actually a member of the Porcellian. And all of them wound up migrating to New York and into Warhol's Factory around the time she did. Edie had found her tribe.

At the same time she was seeing a lot of other people, particularly Bartle Bull. They had met in September at the Casablanca, and from then on they saw each other almost every day all that school year. Whenever our parents came to town, Edie would take him to lunch with them at the Somerset Club, and Fuzzy would show off.

This was the beginning of what Donald Lyons so beautifully called "the brief period of Edie's incandescent openness to life." He said she gave him "the impression of being born just before we met her, and of a raging desire to assimilate as much of life as she could." With all her guileless eagerness, Edie generated a lot of excitement, and it grew and grew until she was the center of attention wherever she went; before long she had amassed a large and miscellaneous entourage. She was, as Suky used to say, all zoom zoom zoom.

But these were the years of wreckage. Edie had not been in Cambridge much more than a month when down in New York Minty had a second and more serious breakdown, and even if my parents tried to keep it from her she must have known, because they were really close. He was picked up by the police wandering around Central Park, so delusional he couldn't even identify himself. Finally, on the basis of the name in the Bible he was carrying, the police were able to reach a cousin of ours, and I must have been away because he called the ranch. It was the same story: my mother said she couldn't do anything just then, and I guess it was the police who took Minty to Bellevue. All I know is that by the time I got to him he was at Manhattan State. I can hardly bear to recall the sight of him in that place, because unlike Bobby, who had been angry and rebellious, he bore it all with the most heartrending dignity. Weeks passed before my parents intervened, and then, against the recommendation of his doctor, they had him taken back to Silver Hill. And that's where he remained all those months, losing ground until finally he gave up hope and took his life. When my father telephoned that night, he said to tell Kate, who was living in New York at the time, and ordered me not to say a word to anyone else until they could get to Cambridge and tell Edie and Suky themselves. They flew east the next day, and when they got to Boston they never even contacted Jonathan; it was Kate who told him on the telephone after I told her. All they thought about was telling Edie and Suky, and when the time came, how did they do it? According to Suky, they told them in the car on the way to the Somerset Club. Suky said she and Edie were in the back seat, and she reacted so violently that she began to scream and Edie had to grab her and hold her down. I asked about Edie, and she said Edie was calm and her response was pure rage, rage against Fuzzy. I had no idea that Minty was gay, but I learned years later that Edie had known for some time because Minty himself had told her. Apparently, he fell in love with somebody, and under pressure he finally came out and told Fuzzy. To me he had described a fight they had one morning in Grandma's apartment, but he never said what it was about. He said he had stood up to Fuzzy and Fuzzy punched him so hard he knocked him down. Minty said that afterward, far from feeling defeated, he felt superior . . . And he *was* superior; he was a superior person in every way. I don't know how Edie bore it when he died, but she did. She was on the rise, and she just kept going, zoom zoom zoom.

Meanwhile, these were years of wreckage in the country at large. All kinds of violence was going on in the South during that fall of 1963, and in Vietnam the US military presence was growing. Then on November 1, the president of the Republic of Vietnam was murdered in an engineered coup, and three weeks later the president of the United States was assassinated while campaigning in Dallas.

Kennedy's assassination seemed to fall on us like a bomb, the shock and sense of disorientation were so enormous. I'm sure Edie heard about it, but I can't imagine she paid much attention. She was too full of her own life. Who hasn't heard the stories: how she was walking along the street with Ed Hennessy, carrying her one book, which was *A Tale of Two Cities* and she took it with her everywhere she went, when a reporter stopped them and asked what they thought of the expression "Better red than dead" and Edie answered without knowing what it meant, and then at somebody's suggestion she told the story to Alger Hiss without knowing who he was; how she took a whole bunch of her friends to the Ritz for lunch and danced on the tables and paid double because she didn't know what to leave for a tip; and how she came into some trust money from Grandma when she turned twenty-one and celebrated her birthday with a famous gala at the Cambridge Boat Club where she danced all night and changed her dress three times. She would dance and dance and then she would break free and dance alone, moving in expressive new ways, completely self-absorbed, just being herself and making a performance of it.

When summer came round, Cambridge emptied for vacation and Edie's entourage dispersed, so the excitement dissipated. She grew restless and wanted to move on. She told everybody she wanted to see what was going on in the wider world, and in July she got Gordon Baldwin to help load all her possessions into the Mercedes and drive with her to New York, where she installed herself in Grandma's apartment at 720 Park Avenue. Bartle Bull was already in town, wanting a change, so right away she went off to Bermuda with him for a week, and when she got back she began frequenting a salon to get her legs reshaped with a view to becoming a model.

It was the summer of 1964. Things were heating up in Vietnam, and in the South the level of violence was rising in response to the campaign to register Black voters. On June 21, three young volunteers named James Chaney, Michael Schwerner, and Andrew Goodman were murdered outside Philadelphia, Mississippi. Less than two weeks later, President Lyndon Johnson signed the Civil Rights Act, and a little over a month after that he signed the Gulf of Tonkin Resolution, auguring war with North Vietnam.

Edie meanwhile was looking around to see what New York might hold for her, and she was in constant touch with her friends from Cambridge. One weekend a beau of hers called John Anthony Walker invited her out to his family's place on Fishers Island, and years later he still remembered every detail of her visit. She missed the ferry from New London and somehow managed to charter a plane, but then the pilot couldn't land in the fog, and yet, hours later there she was, emerging

out of the mist and darkness amid disembodied sounds of rev-
elry, on a yacht that turned out to belong to Jock Whitney.
Knowing how she loved parties, John Anthony took her to
a dance a neighbor was giving in a pavilion near the water,
and the minute Edie began dancing, everybody noticed her,
then she broke free and danced alone out into the night, and
when they followed, there she was under the full moon, turning cartwheels all across the lawn, with the whole sea shin-
ing silver behind her. And the magic didn't end there, because
the next day she disappeared from a picnic on the beach and
nobody could find her until suddenly someone spotted what
looked like a head far out in the water, and it was Edie! She was
playing about in the sea like a dolphin. John Anthony loved her,
he was bewitched by her, but some sense of self-preservation
must have held him back, and eventually they lost touch.

In New York Edie began taking dance classes; during the
day she also tried out for modeling jobs, and at night she went
out, accompanied always by Chuck Wein and a cohort of
Cambridge friends. Right away she began meeting new people and attracting attention, so pretty soon it was zoom zoom
zoom all over again. Social life in New York had always been
more fluid than it was in Boston, and anyway life in the fifties
had been pretty flat and things were beginning to open up.
The privileged young were no longer snobbish and exclusive
the way their elders had been; they were looking for excitement, and they were open to new people from other worlds.
However, there was one domain where there was little interac-
tion, and that was the gay world. The prejudice was still too
powerful. People who considered themselves decent and toler-
ant would speak casually of "fags" and "fairies" and "pansies,"

or describe somebody as "limp-wristed" or "light on his feet." It makes me cringe to remember how we talked. All through the fifties and into the sixties people could not admit openly to being gay, and even if it was understood, their personal and social lives took place out of sight, often in torment and secrecy. In New York, however, the fashion world was quite open, and it was relaxed and glamorous. I had one friend who belonged to it and made no bones about anything. His name was Kenneth Jay Lane, and at that time—this was the late fifties—he was designing shoes. So one evening a bunch of us were having dinner and Ken was full of talk about somebody he had just met, a commercial artist called Andy Warhol who did these great I. Miller ads, and who Ken said had made some lovely drawings of him. I thought he meant portraits, but when the subject came up a couple of years later he said straight out that what Warhol had drawn were his feet and his cock. That's how quickly things changed. One minute you couldn't say anything, the next minute you could—and did— say literally anything.

As the summer progressed Edie got to be more and more of a burden on our grandmother's staff. She was in and out all day, shopping until the closets bulged and all the space under the beds was occupied by boxes from Bendel's and Bergdorf Goodman; she was eating whenever she felt like it and requesting special food, plus she was entertaining her friends, and of course she was out until all hours every night. Pretty soon Grandma's lawyer got wind of it and asked her to leave, so Tommy Goodwin's friend Danny Fields offered to let them both stay at his place, thinking it was just for the weekend. It was a loft over a gyro joint on Twentieth Street between Fifth and Sixth Avenues, quite a change for Miss Edie, but she made herself right at home, using the phone, filling the ashtrays, and helping herself to whatever was around, including any small object she fancied. She was dying to see the World's Fair, so one day they all went, Danny, Tommy, Donald Lyons, Ed Hennessy, and Chuck Wein: five guys and Edie. They took the subway, which was probably a first for her, and at the foot of the concrete steps that led to the World's Fair, she disappeared into the ladies' room and didn't emerge for at least two hours. The others were used to her—they thought she was attending to her makeup—but still it was annoying; nevertheless Danny let her stay for weeks, and long afterward he told Andy Warhol about that time. "The people coming in from Cambridge," Danny said, "always had acid with them—it wasn't even illegal yet . . . It was brown on sugar cubes, and they'd put it in my refrigerator—it looked so harmless, but it was probably enough for two thousand doses. They'd sit at my kitchen table with medicine droppers, bopping their shoulders to the Supremes, dripping the LSD onto the little cocktail sugar cubes. Edie took some acid when she was staying with me, as sort of a debutante giggle." (That's no surprise; Leary and Alpert had come and gone at Harvard a couple of years earlier, and now in Cambridge anyone who wanted it could get LSD.) Another thing Danny said was, "These kids from Cambridge in their early twenties represented inherited wealth, inherited beauty, and inherited intelligence. These were the most glamorous young people in all America . . . [T]hey were *so* rich and *so* beautiful and *so* so smart. And so *crazy*." Edie was completely at ease and in her element among them, so obviously her inexperience made no difference. Anyway, the summer passed, and in September my mother came east and moved her into a small apartment in the East Sixties.

One day early that fall of 1964, I was going to visit my grandmother, who was drifting further and further into dementia, and I was wearing a nice sweater and skirt and my Gucci loafers and, as usual, no makeup. The elevator door opened, and out stepped Edie in a black body stocking, high-heeled boots, and a little fox-fur vest; not only that, she was wearing false eyelashes and the most enormous earrings I had ever seen, made of peacock feathers. I was so shocked. I remember saying, "Is *that* the way you want to go around?" Edie just giggled and said she thought it was fun. Those enormous earrings became her trademark, and guess who designed them? Ken Lane. He had been saying for a while that he wanted to make really big, really lightweight costume jewelry, and now all at once he became a hugely successful designer and a sought-after member of the jet set. Ken told me he owed it all to Edie wearing his earrings.

Edie was completely on her own now. I know she had a psychiatrist, because she was on a regimen of prescription drugs, but I don't know his name or anything about him. What I do know is that she was surrounded by her Cambridge friends, and the closest of them was Chuck Wein, who at this point was devoting himself entirely to Edie, trying to help her establish her life. I also know that the icebox in her new apartment was full of acid, and they were all dropping it. Edie was doing it too, although I'm not sure how much; mainly, she was taking heavy doses of a short-acting barbiturate called Nembutal that the psychiatrist prescribed. So already at this point she was well into drugs; not only that, she was also still stuffing and vomiting. During the day she lived on costly take-out, such as caviar and blinis from Reuben's, and in the evening she and her crowd would go out to one of her favorite restaurants, L'Avventura or the Ginger Man. Edie would order three or four different meals and eat them in succession, leaving the table in between to throw up. (That's something I'll never understand: How come nobody seems to have found that disgusting?) Then she would pick up the bill for everybody and they would all pack into the big gray Mercedes and go somewhere to dance. Edie absolutely loved to drive, and at first she drove herself, even when she was so high on acid she would whiz through lights and over the curb; then she hired Tommy Goodwin and paid him a hundred dollars a week to drive her. That went on until one day Tommy drove into a cab on Park Avenue and wrecked the car; he was worried, but Edie just laughed it off and began calling for limousines. So now she had enormous sleek cars and drivers in livery waiting for her day and night wherever she went. That was pretty conspicuous. Everybody was dazzled by Edie and by her extravagance. She never paid her bills (who *was* paying them? Mummy, surely, and hiding it from our father), and even so she was going through quite a spectacular amount of money. No wonder everyone thought she was an heiress, although in reality she wasn't much of one, any more than she was a real debutante. But there she was, going to more and more parties, more and more clubs and discos, meeting more and more people, dancing with all eyes on her and generating more and more excitement, zoom zoom zoom.

But all this time in private, Tommy Goodwin saw her as "desperate and unhappy, like a caged animal." He said, "[S]he was amoral, a facile liar. She would steal, rob, rip off; she would get herself in awkward situations and lay something on somebody . . . She could bitch and moan and be prissy and infantile, demanding this and that . . . Yet she always had such energy . . . She'd run people ragged. 'Let's go. Let's get into the limo!'" and out they would go into the public eye.

Everywhere she went it was the same thing: when Edie came through the door, the entire atmosphere was electrified; all eyes were on her. That's how magnetic she was. Her circles widened, and now all kinds of people were hearing about this amazing girl and wanting to meet her. So one night in early December, who should ring up out of the blue but that young folk singer Bob Dylan, and Edie called a limousine and went to the Kettle of Fish to meet him. People say they had a big go-round, and it seems pretty clear that those famous songs "Just Like a Woman" and "Leopard-Skin Pill-Box Hat" were written about her, although Dylan denied it all later on, and nobody seems to know what exactly happened between them. I know they were in close touch for quite a time—at one point she even went to stay in Woodstock, which is where Paul Morrissey said she became seriously addicted, presumably to heroin—and there was talk of collaboration. Certainly, she had dealings with Dylan's agent, Albert Grossman, who thought for a time that she might be Hollywood material, and she always said Dylan's friend and collaborator Bob Neuwirth was the great love of her life. But that was many months later, by which time a whole lot else had happened.

Christmastime came round, and Bobby rode his motorcycle down from Cambridge to spend the holiday with Edie, only to find that she had gone home to the ranch after all.

Our parents had told her to come, and they had told him to stay away lest he upset the other children. That's how it happened that Edie was in Santa Barbara on New Year's Eve, driving somewhere with a friend, when she ran a blinking red light just as a big sedan was crossing the intersection. The collision was so horrific they showed it on TV; the car was destroyed, the friend went through the windshield, and Edie smashed her left knee. She also got an ugly cut on her forehead right between the eyebrows. Meanwhile, in New York, on that very same evening at more or less the same time, Bobby was riding his big Harley-Davidson up Eighth Avenue, making sure to catch the lights, riding as always on the very edge, catching every light exactly as it turned . . . until he hit one seconds too soon and rode helmetless into the side of a crosstown bus. He was taken to the hospital, and out in California so was Edie, but she was so scared the accident would give Fuzzy an excuse to put her away that as soon as she was able to leave she persuaded her friend to help fetch her things and drive her directly to the airport in LA. She flew back to New York in a cast that covered her leg from hip to toe.

By the time she got there Bobby had died, and even though our parents told her his death was an accident, she always called it suicide. But suicide was not in Bobby's nature— taking chances was. Whenever I think of his death I think of the time after he broke his neck, when he dreamt that he crawled on his knees to our parents' bedroom door and begged and begged for one more chance, and they told him he had used up all the chances he had. That's it: *no more chances* is all there is to say. Bobby was dead, and Edie kept going, zoom zoom zoom. Death didn't stop her, nor did the huge cast she had on her leg. She needed to dance, and when the cast inter-fered she got somebody to hack it off and replace it with a splint made on the spot out of coat hangers and people's neckties. Then she went right back to the dance floor.

Edie and her crowd were not paying attention, but all this time, the racial situation was worsening: on February 21, Mal-colm X was assassinated by Black Muslims up in Harlem while addressing the Organization of Afro-American Unity. And in Selma, Alabama, on March 7, twenty-five-year-old John Lewis set out at the head of six hundred civil rights protesters to march to the state capitol in Montgomery, which was fifty-four miles away. They never even got out of the city because state troopers beat them back at the Edmund Pettus Bridge, and Lewis had his skull smashed. Two days later, Martin Lu-ther King led two hundred protesters across the bridge, but this time troopers were blocking Highway 80, so they were obliged to halt again, and that night a bunch of white suprem-acists beat a young white minister named James Reeb to even-tual death. Finally, on March 21, several thousand protesters marched out of Selma under the protection of US Army troops and members of the Alabama National Guard, acting on or-ders from President Johnson. When they got to Montgomery four days later, they were joined by a crowd of fifty thousand, and everybody marched together to the state capitol, where Martin Luther King was waiting on the steps to address them. That was on the twenty-fifth of March.

The next day was March 26, and Edie went to a party at a penthouse on East Fifty-Ninth Street, taking Chuck Wein along with her. The host was a successful producer of commer-cials called Lester Persky, who moved in overlapping literary and homosexual circles and liked to give small candlelit dinners for his friends. In this case it was a birthday party for Tennessee Williams, and the reason Edie got invited was that Andy Warhol was coming and Persky knew he was looking for a new star for his films. Everybody knows the outcome: Warhol was smitten at sight. She had that fresh scar on her forehead, but it made no difference; she took his breath away. Somebody heard him say, "Oooh, she's so bee-you-ti-ful," and after they talked he invited her, and Chuck Wein with her, to come to the Factory the next day to see if they might work together.

I had seen my sister a couple of weeks earlier, and that was unusual. Suky was still in Cambridge, but Kate and I were right there in New York, and neither of us ever saw or heard from Edie. She was already in a different world, connected only to our parents, and that mainly because she was always wanting money. So I was surprised and pleased when she came by one evening, bringing a Hello Dolly music box from Tiffany for our little boy, but of course, she didn't stay long. It was the last time I saw her in person, because in April we moved to the Berkshires, and anyway, I was badly shaken by the deaths of my brothers, and I was preoccupied with my own life. But what I did see, and have been seeing ever since, was her image. And now we're getting to the point of all this, because it was as if Edie had stepped straight into the looking glass.

1965

**Andy in the Factory on the couch that Billy Name dragged in**
(Photograph by Stephen Shore)

*Edie had no idea where she was when she entered the Factory, but she had found her way to the one place in the world where for a brief moment she would be fully realized, and to the one person who would take her exactly as she was and catapult the two of them into the empyrean.*

By now everybody has heard about Andy Warhol's Silver Factory, the abandoned hat factory on the north side of East Forty-Seventh Street between Second and Third Avenues. You took the freight elevator to the fourth floor and stepped straight out into a space in which every single surface, even the pay phone by the door, was completely and variously covered in silver. It was fifty by a hundred feet, punctuated by six iron columns, and it had windows and a fire escape at one end and two toilets at the other. At the window end where you came in, you saw the work area where Andy and his assistant Gerard Malanga spent long hours every day turning out Andy's silk-screen paintings. If you arrived in the later afternoon, you would see people milling around behind silver panels toward the back, and of course, the famous couch that Billy Name dragged up from the street, where either a film was being made or people might be hanging out or making out or just attending to their makeup. At the very back, pretty much out of sight except to his friends, people with names like Ondine and Binghamton Birdie and the Sugar Plum Fairy, who came to get amphetamines and listen to his collection of opera recordings, was Billy Name himself, the creator and mainstay of the Silver Factory, who lived there by the toilets, one of which doubled as his darkroom, for, on top of all the other things he did, Billy photographed everything that went on.

So there were two poles in Andy Warhol's Factory, Gerard Malanga at one end and Billy Name at the other. At Gerard's end, the music was mostly rock and roll, and at Billy's it was opera. Billy was a skinny dark-haired guy in his early twenties whose real surname was Linich, but one time when he had to put his name on an *Andy Warhol, Up-Tight* poster, he found it simpler just to put Billy Name, and that stuck. Before that he had been doing lighting off Broadway and living in a place on East Seventh Street that he had covered all over in silver. So one day someone took Andy to one of Billy's famous haircutting parties, and when Andy saw all that silver, right away he wanted that for the hat factory and hired Billy to do it. It took over a year, during which time Billy moved in and he and Andy became really close; for a while that first year they were lovers. Soon it was clear that there was absolutely nothing Billy couldn't do. Not only was he a skilled technician, he also protected Andy, who was inarticulate and shy, by dealing with all the people who wanted his attention, and at one point he even pitched in and painted the basic color on a bunch of Andy's *Boxes*, so Billy became the Factory's unpaid manager.

Gerard Malanga, on the other hand, was a paid employee,

the only one; all the years he worked for Andy he earned $1.25 an hour, and sometimes Andy begrudged him even that. Gerard was an athletic young man with thick tousled curls and classic Mediterranean good looks, and when Andy met him at a party in December 1962 he was not yet twenty and already known in downtown circles as a poet. Then when they met again in June, Andy needed an assistant to help with his silkscreen paintings and Gerard needed a job. It turned out to be a perfect fit. Gerard had worked for a necktie designer printing patterns on thirty-foot lengths of cloth, so he knew all about silk-screen technique, and when it emerged that the reason Andy was pushing the production of his silk-screen paintings was to pay for his films, Gerard got involved in the films as well. He was all energy and enterprise, up for anything, and when the day's work was done, the two of them would go out together. You could say that Gerard gave Andy a whole new social life, because Andy was really shy. Although he would go about uptown with friends to gallery openings and collectors' parties, farther south he hadn't ventured much beyond screenings at the Filmmakers' Cooperative and dance recitals at Judson Memorial Church. Now with Gerard he began going absolutely everywhere—to poetry readings and plays and parties and happenings and screenings and openings and concerts and whatever else was going on wherever it was. And almost every night they went to the movies. So by the following December, when they found the hat factory, Gerard was already part of Andy's life, and in the Factory he came to be known as the prime minister. Basically, you could say that Billy created the conditions for Andy's astonishing productivity and Gerard boosted it, and between the two of them they brought in all kinds of people. As Andy put it, "The way it was working out was that Gerard influenced everything that was away from the Factory, while Billy had gotten to be the main influence at the Factory itself. Gerard kept up with fashion and the arts and he was good at inviting all the celebrities we met to come by the Factory." So right from the start the Factory was an extraordinarily lively and productive place.

## MARCH–APRIL

> BILLY NAME: In '65 the tempo took a change when Edie Sedgwick came in from Boston with her Harvard freaks to be the new Girl of the Year . . . Edie came in like this angel out of a cloud of blue . . . with lightning strikes around her. She was so poised, such a director and actress at the same time . . . When she walked into a room everyone was on point.

Edie had absolutely no idea where she was going.

She hadn't even known who Andy Warhol was, and when Chuck Wein tried to tell her, she said, "What's that? Pop tart?" She told the TV host Merv Griffin when she was on his show, "I came to Andy's studio with a friend, and I didn't know Andy and I didn't really know too much about New York, and he was in the process of making an underground movie, which when I walked in, I couldn't really tell what was happening. There were lots of lights and people running around doing things, and then there were some people huddled together, with more lights on them, and they were sort of making . . .

**Andy looking at Edie** (Photograph by Steve Schapiro)

sounds. And all of a sudden I understood they were reading a
script, and that was part of the movie, and it was in progress.
Well, I just happened to be pushed into a chair in the middle
of it, to sit there, and I didn't really have anything to do with
it, 'cause I never would do it otherwise. And I just sat there
and from that time on I got up the courage to do some more."

The film was called *Vinyl*, and the idea for it had originally
come from Gerard, who got tired of being an extra in Andy's

films and wanted to be the star. For his vehicle he chose *A Clockwork Orange* by Anthony Burgess (and this was years before Kubrick), and Andy claimed he bought the rights for three thousand dollars, which would have been an unthinkable sum for him, who was so careful with money, but then neither Gerard nor Ronnie Tavel, who was Andy's regular scriptwriter at the time, managed to write a screenplay. Instead, Tavel wrote some scenarios and finally came up with a script on the theme of sadomasochism. The cast consisted of five guys—Gerard and another pillar of the Factory who went by the name Ondine, plus an actor, a florist acting the part of the sadistic doctor, and the victim, a boy called Larry Latreille—and filming was underway when in came Edie with her silver-streaked beehive hair, wearing a black tank-top dress and a leopard-skin belt. On an impulse (and to the annoyance of the others), Andy told her to go sit on a trunk right next to the action, just sit there. And that's all she does for most of the film, she just sits there, smoking and occasionally drinking out of a white cup. You can see she doesn't quite know what to do with herself, but then the music takes over and Gerard starts dancing, jumping up and down and thrashing around, and she can't help herself. She begins to sway and move her head, closing her eyes and moving those long white arms about languorously, dancing without ever stirring from her seat. Most of the time she sits there detached, crossing and recrossing her legs, looking on and looking away, smoking and flicking ashes off her cigarette, and all the while some serious S & M stuff is going on right next to her. And afterward, when they saw what they had, there was Edie, completely dominating the screen. You can't take your eyes off her. Ondine said that when they

**Andy filming *Vinyl*** (Photograph by David McCabe)

saw the reruns they got an inkling of what was happening with Edie in the Factory; he said she had a power they hadn't even suspected. As Ronnie Tavel put it, "She ended up stealing the film and becoming a star overnight." But how was Edie to know that what they saw in her was not talent but simply the way she was, transcribed onto the screen?

And is she to be believed when she tells Merv Griffin that was the first time she went to the Factory? Because Ronnie Tavel says Andy merely posed with the movie camera that day so David McCabe could take a picture, and then he walked out, leaving the cameraman Buddy Wirtschafter to take over. According to Tavel, Andy was mad at Gerard, so he was laying into him and deliberately sabotaging the film. And as Tavel complained to Patrick Smith, Andy also sabotaged Tavel himself and his intentions for the film, because the script called for men only, and when Edie showed up, Andy stuck her into the middle of everything. The technical evidence bears Tavel out: at the time it was Andy's practice to keep the camera stationary while shooting; that way he could walk off and let it watch the action for him. In effect, he treated the camera as a surrogate for his eye. However, when Wirtschafter took over, he had to make a sudden adjustment, and that caused it to move. Andy would never have moved it, nor would he have walked out if that had been the very first time Edie Sedgwick showed up at the Factory. However, what I find striking in all this is not just that Edie handled Merv Griffin so artfully, it's something Ronnie Tavel says. He says Andy was going around a lot with "date debutante . . . social register . . . beautiful Edie Sedgwick," and she was bringing him a lot of publicity and attention from the gossip columnists. Wait a minute: They had met on March 26, *Vinyl* was filmed within days of their meeting, and they were already in the gossip columns?

The main thing now, however, was that Edie turned out to be mesmerizing on film, and right away Andy wanted to make a movie that was just about her. It's called *Poor Little Rich Girl*; it was made in the last days of March and the very beginning of April, and it records two reels' worth of her day. I knew the movie was famous, but when I finally saw it I was bewildered, because at first all there was to see was mounds of white foam like bubble bath, heaving and stirring about against a dead-black background. True, there are dark smudges indicating Edie's hair and eyes, so you can keep track of her, although it hardly matters in the beginning because for the first three minutes the camera focuses on her head and face while she sleeps and nothing moves. Then a male voice announces the title and she sits up and gets right on the phone. You hear her talking, asking the time (four o'clock), and chatting a bit. Then she calls and orders five orange juices and, um, two cups of coffee sent up (that's one skill she had, she knew how to order stuff by phone, how to get service so she didn't have to do things for herself). She pulls out a cigarette, lights it, smokes, sits there looking about, and then she must turn something on because suddenly you hear the Everly Brothers singing "Bye Bye Love" and one song after another after that, and sometimes you hear her singing along. What you see is all very blurry, although when she stands up you can tell she's wearing a poufy white dress and when she takes it off it's clear that all she has on is a minuscule black bra and panties. Now she lies on her bed for a minute, bicycles her legs and does some stretches, then she gets up and goes over to her dressing table, finds a cigarette and smokes that, sits down, tries dialing the phone, pours a bunch of pills into her mouth and washes them down with what's left in her cup, and from time to time her head and arms move to the beat. This goes on for a good half hour until eventually the reel runs out—you see that right on the screen—and the numbers of the new one appear and count down. And now suddenly, there's Edie's bare white midriff, navel and all, perfectly distinct, framed top and bottom by her black lace underwear. The camera zooms out to show her sitting on the edge of her bed, and you see she's wearing sheer black tights. Now you really watch, because the camera focuses on her face, and it catches every flicker of expression. I can't get over how enchanting she is. She calls out, "Chuck? Chuck, you going to wake up?" and he wakes up, and for the whole rest of the film the two of them chat, although he remains off-screen. (That's Chuck Wein, who had introduced himself into the filmmaking process and wanted credit as codirector.) Edie fills her pipe from an envelope and asks Chuck if he wants some, but he says, "Not yet." They tell each other their dreams until somebody calls and she talks for a long time and makes faces whenever she has to listen, and now he puts on music that's so loud you can't imagine how she can hear and you can't understand a word she says. Finally, she hangs up and they start chatting again, but the conversation is vague and Edie keeps losing the thread. Anyway, it's hard to make out the words until suddenly she asks, "What am I going to do?" and he says, "Call the bank? . . . Marry somebody rich." She responds that she knows a lot of rich people and they're all pigs; you can't bear to be around them. Then she gives him a charming look and says quite distinctly, "I'd like to kill Grandma, just do away with her." *What?* I've listened to the tape over and over, and I'm quite sure that's what she says, because she giggles and Chuck says something about killing Grandma. Edie just laughs and fills her pipe. At one point she tells him, "Mummy says they're not going to give me another penny, not even for medicine." (But they did, they always did, or rather Mummy did. God only knows what it cost her.) They talk some more, and after a while he says to her quite matter-of-factly, "I think you should get sick in front of everybody," and I thought I heard her say that way she doesn't get fat. (Doesn't she realize he's causing her to put her whole self on display? Doesn't she mind?) Now she stands up and goes to the closet, pulls out the famous leopard-skin coat, and puts it on over her underwear to show him. "It's the most beautiful coat in the world," she says, and explains that it was a gift from a funny Englishman, the one who wanted to give her a lot of money. She takes the coat off, wriggles out of her leopard-skin belt without mussing her beehive hair, and picks up a sleeveless white jumpsuit that she steps into and ties the sash around her hips, so you realize she's getting ready to go out. She fishes out a very long chain with a locket, puts it on, and starts rummaging in something out of sight where she says with a sly look that she put a hundred-dollar bill, then she gives up and dabs perfume all round her neck. Chuck tells her to try calling Dominic, he's going into the other room, and suddenly you hear his voice announcing the title and credits, and that's the end. It turned out that the lens of the camera had not functioned correctly the first time, so Andy shot another version that doesn't have the defect and combined the two, putting the blurry part first, because that was what he was like. He set it all up and then he dealt with what came. Andy said if Edie had needed a script, she wouldn't have been right for the part, which tells you something else about his approach to filmmaking. It also tells you something about Edie: she could never be anything but herself, and as herself she was absolutely riveting on-screen. When Jonas Mekas saw the film, he was impressed: he wrote that *"Poor Little Rich Girl*, in which Andy Warhol records seventy minutes of Edie Sedgwick's life, surpasses everything that the cinema verité has done till now." But Edie didn't see it that way: when it was screened at the Cinematheque on April 26, she walked out, convinced that she had been made to look ridiculous.

Andy was transfixed by her. Many years later he wrote, "One person in the 60s fascinated me more than anybody I had ever known. And the fascination I experienced was probably very close to a certain kind of love." For Andy this is an extraordinary admission, given his evasiveness, his reflexive nonchalance when it came to anything even remotely personal. He adds that she had more problems than anyone he'd ever met, and it occurs to me that he might be defending himself, because by then she was dead of an overdose and a lot of people blamed him for what happened to her. However, there is no question that at the beginning and throughout their first months together, Edie was a wonder in his eyes and, whatever that might mean in his case, he certainly appeared to be in love. There's no other word for it. Just look at that photograph by Steve Schapiro: there's Edie in profile looking eagerly straight ahead, and Andy is gazing at her with his head on one side, completely moonstruck. I think the photograph says a lot about their relationship: he's gazing at her and she's looking to see what's ahead for her. "Love" is not a word I would associate with Edie; what she wanted more than anything was the intense experience of life. She wanted what she called "action," and while nobody would necessarily have described Andy as "exciting," given his vague elusive manner and recessive presence, he generated a huge amount of energy around him, and the Factory was a very exciting place to be. More important, Edie was instantly and deeply engaged by the camera, and she must have sensed Andy capturing her. The fact that he thought she was so good on film gave her validation and a focus, neither of which she had ever experienced before; clearly, she felt herself to be affirmed.

Another thing that's clear is that there was a deep sense of complementarity between them. For instance, when they met

Edie was already spraying silver streaks in her hair because she liked the look of light hair with dark eyes, and he was already wearing a gray wig to make himself look young, but now he sprayed his hair to match hers. He told Old Owl (i.e., the very young Robert Reilly, Old Owl being the mascot of the Yale *Record*) in an interview, "Edie's hair was dyed silver, and therefore I copied my hair [*sic*] because I wanted to look like Edie because I always wanted to look like a girl." And when they returned from Paris it was she who cut her hair short like his and dyed it completely silver. Think how liberating it must have been for Andy, shy and socially insecure as he was, to go about with a beautiful sought-after girl who looked like a glamorous version of him. From the day she came through the door and for most of that year, the two of them were inseparable, and when they were not together they would talk for endless hours on the phone. Edie took Andy with her to all the glamorous parties and fashionable bars and discotheques that she frequented, and he took her into the art world, to gallery openings and events and the parties that his collectors, people like the Sculls and the Tremaines, gave to show off their acquisitions. One night Jacques Kaplan, the furrier-turned-dealer, gave a party, and McCabe's photographs show Edie there in Kaplan's closet, holding her own in the company of artists like Wynn Chamberlain and Larry Poons while Henry Geldzahler leaned against the wall and smoked his cigar. Above all, what Edie liked was an arena in which to shine, and now wherever they went, she and Andy really shone.

Their first taste of blockbuster celebrity as a couple came almost at once, on April 9, when they went to the preview of the exhibition *Three Centuries of American Painting* at the

Metropolitan Museum and drew more attention than the First Lady of the United States, Lady Bird Johnson, who was the guest of honor. Imagine the scene: Andy in his untidy wig, a beat-up tuxedo jacket, and the pants he wore to paint in, Edie with silvery hair and enormous Ken Lane earrings, in nothing but a body stocking and lavender jersey pajamas, and everybody else uptight in their costly conventional finery. It was the first glimpse Andy got of Edie's power to draw attention in a crowd, and it was the first glimpse that both the patriciate and the public at large got of the two of them.

The same thing happened at the Factory on April 25, when Lester Persky gave his famous Fifty Most Beautiful People Party there. That was the occasion when New York society and the jet set and the whole glittering world of fashion and celebrity entered the gay and druggy underworld, and both the Factory and society itself were transformed by the encounter. Edie was there, mussing Brian Jones's hair and looking beautiful, according to Andy, and whether it was just her or because *Vinyl* was screened during the party, it seems more people stared at her than they did at all the celebrities. And that included Judy Garland, who was completely out of control and shrieking from the moment she rode out of the elevator on the interlocked arms of Persky and Tennessee Williams until long after the party ended the following day.

Andy needed to fly to Paris with Gerard Malanga at the end of the month to install the exhibition of his *Flowers* at Ileana Sonnabend's gallery, and now he invited Chuck Wein and Edie to come along. He and Edie had gotten a lot of attention in the press for the opening at the Met, and he wanted to see what would happen in Paris. He thought, and Ileana

Sonnabend thought so too, that it was helpful for an artist to appear with a beautiful woman on his arm. As for Edie, you'd think she would be excited because, except for that disastrous overnight in Vienna, she had never been to Europe, and now here she was, going to Paris, but somehow Edie always seemed to take everything in stride and look for the next thing. She had already begun wearing a T-shirt over a leotard and tights, nothing to do with fashion, she said, but simply because her parents had severely limited her funds, and Andy says that's what she had on when she got off the plane, a T-shirt and tights, and over her shoulder, a white mink coat. He says she wore that the whole time she was there, because she had packed almost nothing else, except for a second white mink coat just in case. You might want to take what he says with a grain of salt, though, because McCabe photographed them all in the taxi on the way to the airport, and Edie had on a sleeveless black jersey dress, sheer stockings, and her tall high-heeled boots; moreover, that mink coat was made of tails. But who knows, she might have changed on the plane, because she definitely did wear her leotards in Paris—she says so on the soundtrack of *Afternoon*.

Pop Art was percolating in Paris. Sonnabend had shown some of Andy's *Death and Disaster* pictures the previous year, and now both the press and the public were avidly anticipating his arrival. So the stage was set. The reception of the *Flowers* show exceeded everyone's expectations, and the response of critics and public alike was extraordinary. Peter Schjeldahl wrote, "It was as if, in a dark, grey atmosphere, someone had kicked open a blast furnace. The beauty, raciness, and cruelty of those pictures—an insipid pansy image negligently silkscreened in chemical colors—seemed to answer a question so big I could never have hoped to ask it." Andy gave lots of interviews, he and Edie were photographed as a couple for *Vogue* and *Paris Match*, and the two of them were lionized wherever they went. Steven Watson describes them at the Crazy Horse Saloon with Salvador Dalí the day after the opening: "A spotlight directed on the table indicated the presence of celebrity, and loudspeakers announced the joint presence of the father of Surrealism and the father of Pop. Dalí bowed and basked in the attention, while Warhol squirmed, and Edie leaned over to ask Dalí how it felt to be a famous writer." She really didn't know a thing, and it never mattered a bit. Andy must have loved that about her. Certainly, at this point they flourished in each other's company, and Gerard and Chuck Wein flourished along with them, although I read somewhere that Gerard's diary was full of complaints about the influence Edie was having on Andy. Andy, however, was having such a good time, and he liked Paris so much, that he decided to make the big announcement he'd been thinking about: he was going to retire from painting. He said later, "Art just wasn't any fun for me anymore; it was people who were fascinating and I wanted to spend all my time being around them, listening to them, and making movies of them."

From Paris the four of them went to London for a day or two, and before returning to New York and the Factory, they spent a lavish week at the Hotel El Minzah in Tangiers, where everyone but Andy was happy about all the drugs and he thought the city stank of piss and shit. It was his first vacation in nearly ten years. Then when they got back to New York, Edie established her look. She got Billy Name to cut her hair off—I think he was the one who cut it from then on, because once they did it out on the Factory fire escape and Ondine held the microphone while Andy filmed the scene—and then she dyed it silver and began going everywhere dressed in a leotard and tights. She was Andy's recognized consort and the undisputed queen of the Factory, where it seems absolutely everybody, gay or straight, was in love with her.

In fact, at that particular point in both their lives Edie really suited all Andy's purposes. Publicity, to begin with. He had always been so preoccupied with it that early on he engaged a press agent and consulted him daily, telling him everything he had done, which was unheard-of for an artist at the time, and in 1964 he hired the young British fashion photographer David McCabe to follow him for an entire year and document his life, particularly his presence at social events around town. McCabe said he hadn't even known who Andy Warhol was: "At that time he had a certain notoriety in Manhattan, but he wasn't famous the way he would later become. All that changed in the year I was photographing him." When the year was up, McCabe showed Warhol the photographs, and it seems he pored over the contacts with a magnifying glass, not to choose prints but to study the way he was presenting himself to the world. In other words, what interested him was not the pictures but his image. He was consciously re-creating himself. McCabe said, "[A]t the beginning of the year he was very smiley and open, very normal. By the end, he had his sunglasses on—he'd adopted this mysterious, noncommunicative persona." It was during this period of transformation that Edie came into his life, and now the press took notice of every least move the two of them made.

All his life, fame had been Andy's main preoccupation, and it had been a long time coming. As a commercial artist he had started out in the gay fashion scene, which had its limitations, and he had had a hard time breaking into the art world, although things had been going better since his first two real exhibitions. In July 1962, Irving Blum showed *Campbell's Soup Cans* at the Ferus Gallery in LA, and in November Eleanor Ward showed a bit of everything—*Soup Cans* and *Coke Bottles* and *Marilyns* and the *Dance Diagram*, even an early *Death and Disaster*—at the Stable Gallery in New York. Both exhibitions got a lot of attention, much of it negative. David Bourdon saw Andy at the party after the opening at the Stable and described how uncomfortable he was: "[H]e just stood against the wall and said almost nothing at all. It was partly because he was terrorized by the art world. He was fairly famous as a commercial designer, and a lot of the people who turned up to that first show came to be resentful and vindictive and to see what he was really up to. He was really trying to make it in the art world, and he was terrified  . . ." But then in April 1964, Ward gave him that notorious show of *Boxes*, and after that Andy was in a position to leave her for the most prominent dealer in contemporary art in New York, Leo Castelli. So now he was on his way to real success. And at the same time, thanks to the enthusiasm of Jonas Mekas, he was being recognized for his underground films. However, welcome as all this was, when Edie entered his life, Andy was still light-years away from the glamorous world he aspired to, the world of celebrities and high society. All his life, going back to the time when he was a sick little boy in bed in Pittsburgh looking at movie magazines and writing away to Shirley Temple, he had been obsessed with stars and celebrities; more than anything in the world, he longed to be admitted into their company. However, he was painfully shy, and he was self-conscious about his looks. With some justification: his skin was blotchy and prone to pimples, his nose was red and lumpy, and he wore that peculiar wig. On top of it all, his manner was unabashedly "swish" (I know that word is offensive, but that's the way everybody talked in those days). To give you an idea what he was up against, here's how the socialite photographer and psychotherapist Frederick Eberstadt described him as he was around 1960, when he was trying to break into the art world: "Here was this cooley [sic] little faggot with his impossible wig and his jeans and his sneakers and he was sitting there telling me that he wanted to be as famous as the Queen of England! It was embarrassing. Didn't he know that he was a creep? In fact, he was about the most colossal creep I had ever seen in my life. I thought that Andy was lucky that anybody would talk to him." And now suddenly, here he was entering all doors with a beautiful and very conspicuous society girl who looked and dressed just like him. The two of them were inseparable, and soon they were the most sought-after couple in town. No event, however grand and exclusive, was a success unless they were there. People even sent limousines to be sure they came. What's more, Edie no sooner arrived at one party than she was ready to move on to the next, so they would go through four or five a night. And to Andy that signified glamour. With Edie at his side he suddenly found that he had become glamorous; together, they were a super-glamorous pair, and Andy's public image was transformed, although I suspect he didn't quite believe it yet. What mattered to him was that now he had an entrée, and that's what Edie provided. The poet Charles Henri Ford was once asked what ultimate success meant to Andy, whether it was money, and his immediate response was, "Publicity and glamour." Ford recalled putting the same question to Gerard Malanga, and Gerard had said what Andy really wanted was glamour. Ford asked if he'd gotten it, and Gerard's answer was, "He's getting it."

But what Andy was most interested in doing now was making movies, so in the immediate sense perhaps the most important thing about Edie was how good she was on camera. Here's what he said about her: "Edie was incredible . . . just the way she moved. And she never stopped moving for a second—even when she was sleeping, her hands were wide awake. She was all energy—she didn't know what to do with it when it came to living her life, but it was wonderful to film. The great stars are the ones who are doing something you can watch every second, even if it's just a movement inside their eye." And that's precisely the quality she had: on film she is so intensely alive that even when she's just sitting there apparently doing nothing, you watch her. Everything about her is active. She's looking down, her head flies up in response to something; those big sooty eyes widen, narrow, and widen again; she smiles and dimples appear, but now she suddenly makes a face, frowns, cocks her head and looks inquiring, amazed, skeptical . . . She takes a drag on her cigarette and leans forward, letting out the smoke; she looks up and asks for something, and all the time she's arranging and rearranging those long long legs, making sure they appear to advantage. You know where you can really see how Edie engaged with the lens? There's a screen test where she appears with a faun-like

Slavic-looking boy whom Andy was trying out to see if there was any chemistry between them. The boy is close beside Edie but deeper in the space, and he looks at her, attempting to reach her; you can see him yearning for her to relate to him . . . but he might as well not be there at all, because she is wholly intent on the camera. She comes through the lens like a fist, and all you see on the film is Edie engaging with the eye that's on her.

Another thing about Edie: she really lit up the Factory. You can tell from the pictures that she was the center of everything; you can see how enchanting she was, how happy and engaged. She absolutely loved to dance; it's as if she needed to—you see it in *Vinyl* and again in *Poor Little Rich Girl*, how her whole body responds almost involuntarily to the sound and beat of music—and that was infectious, so now you see all kinds of people twisting and frugging and leaping about, and there's Edie suavely doing her signature moves in her white silk tunic or her leotard and tights and stiletto heels. Plus, she was cozy and playful, and she could tease Andy and draw him out of his shyness; once she even dragged him into a pool with all his clothes on, and there they were, paddling about, he in his striped cotton top and she in her tiny black lace bra and panties, both of them with matted silver hair. Those boat-necked striped tops are the emblem of Edie's time in the Factory; she wore them over leotards and tights, and Andy wore them with tight black pants instead of his old jeans. Gerard and Chuck wore them too, only Edie's let you see her arms.

Chuck Wein was right in there with Edie in the Factory. She always referred to him as her advisor, others called him a cross between Svengali and a nursemaid, and he was all that and more. He was her most intimate and inseparable

Edie and Donald Lyons dancing in the Factory; Dorothy Dean,
Chuck Wein, and others in the background (Photograph by Stephen Shore)

companion, and because he was the one who could activate
her on film, he got involved in every movie Andy made with
her and wanted credit as codirector. Chuck had his elbows
out, and that caused tension as he impinged on the role of
Ronnie Tavel and even on Gerard's position in the hierarchy. The other members of Edie's Cambridge group who had
drifted into the Factory—Ed Hood, Gordon Baldwin, Tommy
Goodwin, Donald Lyons, Ed Hennessy, and a girl named

142

Sandy Kirkland—mostly just hung around the sidelines, and appeared now and then in Andy's films. There were two older figures from Harvard who were more central: one was Arthur Loeb, an eccentric offshoot of the New York investment banking family, and to my astonishment, the other was Dorothy Dean, who I had heard was in Cambridge typing and editing Professor Sidney Freedberg's big manuscript on sixteenth-century Italian painting. You can see them all in photographs: Chuck, ever the dandy, sometimes all in white, sometimes in a striped top like Andy and Edie, the others in suits and ties, and Dorothy in a skirt looking like a Radcliffe girl, all of them sitting or standing around when they're not romping about to the music. In fact, for a time the Cambridge crew were such a presence in the Factory that they virtually eclipsed the other habitués, all the drag queens and outlandish misfits that Andy gathered and the gay opera lovers and A-men and Mole People, the nocturnal speed freaks who frequented Billy Name.

"Joy" is the word that Edie's Cambridge friend Donald Lyons used to describe the life he knew in the Factory; he said it was "a perpetual dance party  .  .  .  , a perpetual party in one place or another  .  .  .  , so that there was an opportunity to endlessly experience the sense of life as a joy." It's also the word he used to describe what Edie was looking for: "It's not that she wanted the next party, she wanted the next joy." However, there's no mention of joy in the interview that Lyons did with Lynne Tillman. There he talks about the dandyism, all the extravagance, the tremendous energy put into style rather than sex, and the interpenetration of high and low and gay and straight. To my surprise he says he found the Factory tawdry, but a good place to hang out in the afternoon until the parties began. On the subject of drugs he says amphetamines were the main thing, that Factory regulars like Ondine and Brigid Polk were going off in the bathroom all the time, but that the Cambridge group was not involved; all they would take was a little pop of speed or hashish before setting forth on their evening rounds . . . He says the Cambridge years in the Factory were not driven by drugs, although, he says, Edie's story was different and he doesn't want to go into it.

In time the Cambridge people vanished from the Silver Factory, but Brigid Polk and Ondine were at the center of it as long as it lasted. Brigid was a big, hefty girl with bushy hair, and I think she was probably Andy's best friend throughout his life; they spoke on the phone for hours every day, and she was the "B" to his "A" in his *Philosophy from A to B*. However, she didn't start out as part of his circle; she came into the Factory pursuing the dealer they called Rotten Rita, who she had a big crush on even though he was most definitely gay, and she went straight through to the back, where Ondine and the other Mole People were sitting around, high on amphetamines, listening to Billy Name's opera LPs and commenting on the performances. Brigid's real surname was Berlin (her father was Richard Berlin, the president and CEO of the Hearst Corporation), but she called herself Brigid Polk because she would give absolutely anybody—including herself—a poke in the fanny right through the pants. In the Factory she was known as the Duchess because of her social position and her society-lady accent, inherited from what sounds like a monster of a society-lady mother. As for Ondine, his real name was Robert Oliva, and he had entered the Factory with Billy Name, along with some of Billy's other friends, the so-called amphetamine rapture group, who kept Billy company during the many months it took him to turn the dingy old space silver, and simply stayed on. In the words of Andy's friend and biographer Victor Bockris, Ondine was "a self-described 'running, standing, jumping drug addict' and a brilliant verbal acrobat." Bockris says Andy, who was himself so silent, was fascinated by Ondine's verbal extravagance, and he quotes Billy Name, who told him, "Ondine was not just that verbalist crazy person, he was a high-powered intellect." But Ondine was a lot more even than that: he was a true comic, and his timing was flawless. Here's just one example, as described by Andy:

> David Whitney . . . stepped out of the elevator with two very suburban women from Connecticut who were "interested" in my art. I was standing there doing some Flowers for my Paris show coming up in May and talking to the women when Ondine came out from the back holding a huge jar of Vaseline and launched into a whole big tirade against drag queens and transvestites, maintaining that if you couldn't do whatever you wanted to without *any* clothes on—*least* of all women's—then you should forget about sex altogether.

Ondine was also terrific on film, and that was Andy's main interest now, and his principal activity.

## MAY–JUNE

A day or so before the trip to Paris, Andy had attended a session at Jonas Mekas's Filmmakers' Cooperative, where a seventeen-year-old photographer named Stephen Shore was showing his 16 mm film *Elevator*. Shore went up to Andy afterward and asked whether he would mind if he came and took pictures at the Factory. Andy said he was just leaving for Paris but would get in touch when he got back, and Shore thought that might be the end of it. But now, one evening in late May, he got a call from Andy saying they were filming at that restaurant called L'Avventura and would he like to come and take pictures? Shore went straight over and took a bunch of photographs, then he followed everybody back to the Factory, and for most of the next two years he went there almost every day. The film was *Restaurant*.

Unlike the previous two movies that Edie had appeared in, this one is pretty conventional, because it simply shows her dining at L'Avventura with Ondine and a group of Cambridge friends: Ed Hennessy, Ed Hood, Donald Lyons, Dorothy Dean, and Sandy Kirkland. It's shot in those chalky whites and velvet blacks that are so very flattering to Edie, and when it opens, the camera is trained from a low angle on the end of a table and a still life of bottles, glasses, and a large Cinzano ashtray. We hear people talking, we see a hand picking up glasses and tapping the ashes off a cigarette, and eventually, very gradually, the camera zooms out until there's Edie sitting at the right, wearing a black leotard and a whole lot of metal: her trademark dangly earrings, plus a long studded chain that's looped ten times around her neck and another, rather suggestive chain that passes around her midriff and encircles each of her bare arms above the elbow. She's talking mostly across the table to Donald Lyons, while Ondine sits beside her giving off a huge vibe of mischief and charm. In fact, Ondine exerts

146

almost as big a pull on the lens as Edie does, although she's the one doing most of the talking. Her conversation is not at all vague, and she doesn't lose the thread, although from time to time she interrupts herself to lean back and ask the waiter rather imperiously to bring her another drink—I think she says it's vodka. (That was a surprise; I knew about the drugs, but I had no idea she drank.) What is interesting to me is how very self-possessed she seems, how completely at ease and in command, and as always, how wonderfully alive. As she talks she's constantly smoking, drawing hard on the cigarette and blowing out the smoke, and all the while she's moving her lovely white arms about and arranging and rearranging those long legs in response to the gaze of the lens. At a certain point, I thought I heard her complain that somebody had caused her to make a public fool of herself; I didn't catch who it was, but it shows how mistrustful Edie was right from the start.

I don't know what caused Edie's misgivings, whether it was her own inner sense of herself or her ignorance of the world making her suspicious, but another factor might be that in the social circles she frequented uptown, most people didn't understand any better than she did what it meant to be the star of Andy Warhol's underground films. One thing is clear: Edie was happy to be a star, she just wasn't sure a Warhol superstar was the real thing. She needed to believe that what she was doing was real, and with Andy she could never be confident. You have to remember that she had not grown up going to movies; there was no television on the ranch and no movie theater within forty miles. So it's not surprising that she didn't know what to make of his films, and given the factor of camp, a lot of them must have looked pretty unconvincing to her.

Her next film was *Kitchen*, and apart from the screen tests they were making right along (by the end there were nine of them), this was the sixth film Andy had made with Edie in a two-month period. Apart from the three I've mentioned, there were two others, both of which are now lost. The one called *Bitch* was made at the same time as *Vinyl*, and she only had a small part in it, but the one called *Face* was just about her. According to Jonas Mekas, it was seventy minutes long, black-and-white, with sound, filmed sometime in April, and it was a long close-up of Edie's face, related to *Poor Little Rich Girl*. *Kitchen*, however, was a more ambitious film, and it was much admired when it was screened at the Cinematheque on March 3, 1966. The instructions that Andy gave Ronnie Tavel are well known: he wanted a script for Edie, something in a kitchen . . . white and clean and plastic . . . no plot, just a situation. The location is also known. It was the kitchen of the cameraman Buddy Wirtschafter's apartment, a cramped space, all white, with a table in the middle. The cast consisted of Edie, Roger Trudeau, Donald Lyons, Elektrah, René Ricard as the houseboy, and David McCabe playing himself as the photographer who moves in and out taking pictures. Tavel had given Edie a script, and he wanted to hold rehearsals, but she was quite incapable of memorizing lines, plus Chuck got her stoned and kept her out late the night before the shooting, some said because he didn't believe in lines, others because he was trying to undermine Tavel. So in the end Edie's lines were written out on cards and planted all over the set, and she was supposed to sneeze whenever she needed prompting. She sneezes so often that when Norman Mailer was asked years later to comment on the film, he recalled the dreadful cold

Edie in Andy Warhol, *Kitchen*, 1965
(16 mm film, black and white, sound, 66 minutes)

she had. Basically, the action consists of Edie coming in and sitting at the table in her striped top and fishnet stockings while the others mill around, and you can tell she's feeling that lens on her legs—just look how consciously she keeps moving and arranging them. Meanwhile, everybody's chatting, they're all busy with this and that, at one point somebody turns on a really noisy kitchen appliance, and in the end they lay Edie out on the table and throttle her.

Characteristically, Mailer saw all this as portentous and thumped his chest. He said, "[A] hundred years from now people will look at *Kitchen* and say, 'Yes, that is the way it was in the late Fifties, early Sixties in America. That's why they had the war in Vietnam. That's why the rivers were getting polluted. That's why there was typological glut. That's why the horror came down. That's why the plague was on its way.'" Andy and Ronnie Tavel, however, looked at their film quite differently. Andy thought it was Tavel's best script, and Tavel thought one reason their collaboration worked so well was that their approaches were so compatible: as a playwright, he thought in terms of the stage, and Andy for his part used a fixed camera and didn't believe in editing. When Tavel was asked to explain *Kitchen*, he said the point was to unsettle the audience, to deprive them of a sense of reality and keep them questioning what it was they were seeing: *"What are they doing? What is this about? Are they making a film or are they rehearsing a play or are they just crapping around?"* He went on to say, "The final mind-fuck is the ending . . . You sit there and think *Well, it's obviously a fake ending. They just have to get this over with so they're killing the lead.* But on the other hand, you're forced to confess that that kind of behavior will lead to murder, and this is a final parody; it's fake and it's real and it's a perfect equation." And if you want to know what Edie made of it, she simply dismissed it. She asked Tavel what the film was supposed to mean, and when he told her he hoped it meant nothing, she responded that she didn't know what that meant; it didn't mean anything. And a few days later, when Tavel showed them his script for *Shower*, Andy merely said he didn't understand it, but Edie scorned it. She told Tavel that he was capable of something better, that that kind of thing wasn't worthy of him.

Edie could be equally high-handed with Andy himself. There's a tape of her talking to him about some film they were planning, I don't know which, and she says, "I mean, what's your concern, just a nothing?" Andy says, "No, but—" and she interrupts him: "Like, just a bunch of people? Who cares?" She talks with real authority, as if she knows what's what. And that's nothing compared to what she said to Merv Griffin when she and Andy were interviewed on his show. If you see the video, you can tell right away that Griffin means to have fun with the two of them for the benefit of the audience, because here's how he introduces them: "Pop Art, Op Art, underground movies, call it what you will, these two are the leaders. No party is considered a success unless they are there," and then he brings them in to the tune of "Pop Goes the Weasel." Edie's wearing a demure little black jacket with a lace collar on top of a leotard and sheer black tights, and Andy appears in a dark suit, carrying a leather satchel. Once they're settled in their chairs, Edie at Griffin's right and Andy between her and a chunky blond comedienne who's already in place, Griffin turns toward them and, after some banter about Edie's jacket, greets Andy, who merely nods. Her hands moving nonstop, Edie explains to Griffin in her very innocent, girlish way that Andy is not used to public appearances, so when he gets a direct question he will whisper to her and she will pass on what he says. Griffin then begins the interview by asking somewhat snidely what underground movies are. The question is put to Andy, but now something unexpected happens (and incidentally, it's a device that Andy discovered once when he was struggling during an interview on WBAI and Henry Geldzahler intervened to explain what he meant): Andy punts to Edie, and she takes charge. So far, she tells Griffin firmly, these underground movies have been visual experiments, people making movies trying to see if they can do it. Griffin asks about the subject matter, probably planning to get a big laugh from the audience when they hear what some of these films are about, and Edie looks around rather archly, confesses that she doesn't dare say it, and launches into a description of *Sleep*. It's a fabulous movie, she says, that Andy made of somebody sleeping, for eight hours, was it? Andy gives a minimal nod, and she goes on, "[A]nd the camera's on somebody and all they're doing is sleeping—well, you can see them *breathing*." Brilliant. She has Merv Griffin right where she wants him—what can he do with that? He asks meekly whether it takes eight hours to watch it, and she brushes the question aside, and now just listen to what she says: "Well, . . . that was all before *I* got in on it. Um, now it's all changed . . . We have other influences, and we're going to have a big production, a real thing." She describes the project, which won't be eight hours long, only one and a half, and it's *Jane Eyre*, a modern version, "somewhat spacey, and, um, using a plot but putting it into a modern context." And here she almost loses control, because Merv Griffin says, "*Really!*" and that gives the blond comedienne her opening. She leans right across Andy and asks Edie if she is going to play Jane. When Edie says she is, the comedienne says, "Then I could play Air," and looks round at the audience. That gets a big laugh. A bit of horsing around ensues, and Griffin's cohost pretends to snore. But Edie knows how to stop a runaway. "That's a drag!" she says loud and clear. "I don't want to hear any more of that." And she's right back on top.

Griffin tries again. He says to Edie, "Now, you are a superstar, or you want to be a superstar . . . What is the difference between a star and a superstar?" and Edie tells him straight: "It's two things. One is a *joke* and the other is possibly a real superstar . . . if there could be such a thing." Griffin presses on, and when after a bit he asks her to define "superstar," she responds: "Something either fantastic or ridiculous, and that remains to be seen." She wags her finger, and now she says, quite emphatically, "It *may be* ridiculous. If we can't get it off the ground it'll be ridiculous." So there you have what Edie thinks Andy Warhol's underground movies are and how she regards her role in making them, including her reservations. Two things about the interview really surprised me: first of all, how masterfully Edie handled it, and second, that she obviously believed she was raising Andy's filmmaking to a whole new level. As for Andy, he looked perfectly pleased with the way it all went.

I doubt very much if Edie knew anything at all about the technical side of filmmaking (not that Andy himself knew much), and I cannot imagine that she knew anything about

**Edie talking to Andy in the Factory** (Photograph by Stephen Shore)

*Sleep*. To begin with, it was only five and a half hours long, and the idea had come to Andy during a long night spent watching his lover John Giorno while he slept. They were staying at Eleanor Ward's place in the country that weekend in the summer of '63, when Jack Smith was making kind of a sequel to *Flaming Creatures*, and all sorts of people were there participating. Even Antonioni came to watch. Andy had brought along a borrowed 16mm Bolex, and he not only filmed some of the action for himself, he took a lot else from Jack Smith and the whole experience, including the term "superstar" and a bunch of actors, among them the great female impersonator Mario Montez. What Edie did know something about were the films that she and Chuck planned with Andy, where she had some input and Andy treated her as an equal, but as for the rest, you heard what she said to Ronnie Tavel about *Kitchen*.

The costume that Edie wears in *Kitchen* was what she wore pretty much everywhere now, a top over a leotard and tights, and sometimes she didn't even bother with the top. This was partly because she was taking dance classes, partly because she was short of money, but mainly because those were the clothes she was happiest in, and now the fashion world began to take notice. The magazines had been aware of Pop Art right along, and they had been using it as props and backgrounds for shoots. In mid-April, for instance, *Mademoiselle* had commissioned David McCabe to do a Pop world fashion shoot featuring Andy and an entourage. The entourage consisted of Edie, Gerard Malanga, and Chuck Wein, and McCabe photographed them in his studio, all stacked up with their arms out and bent so they look like a totem pole of the multi-armed Hindu god Shiva: Edie cross-legged on the floor in front, Gerard right behind her, then Chuck, and Andy at the top. Edie still had her big beehive, which was sprayed silver, and she was wearing a black turtleneck sweater, heavy black tights, and knee-high black boots with high heels. Oh, and no earrings. Andy and Gerard were in proper suits, and Chuck had on a white fisherman's sweater. So it was early days. But by the end of the month Edie was wearing her dance clothes more and more, and she caught the eye of a rising fashion designer her same age named Betsey Johnson. Betsey had started out as a teenager making outfits for her school dance recitals, and now she was interested in designing clothes that had some of the same feel. She was working at *Mademoiselle* at that point, and on the side she was creating custom-made silver clothes for various clients in the fashion world, using Edie as her fitting model. One day late that spring, Edie asked if she could borrow some samples, or rather, someone called from the Factory and asked her to send over all her silver stuff. So Betsey sent her silver knits, her metallic and glitter silvers, all she had, for Edie to choose from.

Edie chose the silver crushed-velvet jumpsuit you see her wearing in the extraordinary photograph that David McCabe took of her and Andy on the roof of his building. It looks like a Soviet Socialist Realist poster, those inspirational images of workers looking toward a radiant future: they're seen from below standing on a metal ladder, gazing outward heroically with their arms stretching up to the skies and the Empire State Building soaring in the background. The image is so astonishing, so perfectly composed, that you are stunned; you don't even notice the possible allusion to Andy's film *Empire*, which really was eight hours long, and it never enters your mind that this picture is pure camp. To me it marks the beginning of the high season of Edie Sedgwick and Andy Warhol.

## JULY–AUGUST

*Kitchen* was a critical success in the underground movie world, and so was the next film in the series about Edie, which they made in mid-July. It's called *Afternoon*, and what it shows is Edie and friends—Ondine, Arthur Loeb, Dorothy Dean, and Donald Lyons—whiling the time away together in Edie's apartment at 16 East Sixty-Third Street, talking and smoking to the accompaniment of vodka and amphetamines. The whole film seems really spontaneous, so I was surprised to learn that quite a lot of planning went into it, and a lot of discussion among Andy and Edie and Chuck Wein. The first time I saw it I couldn't make out much of the dialogue; it was not until I read the transcript that the whole film came to life for me, and I was reminded of those private entertainments that used to take place in aristocratic houses. *Afternoon* is like a chamber opera, in which Edie, posed on the sofa charming as ever in her black leotard, a silky black top, and sheer tights, plays the presiding spirit, and Dorothy and Donald serve as the chorus, while Ondine and Arthur Loeb engage in an endless duet and Andy helps the plot along from the prompter's box, which he shares with the inevitable Chuck Wein. See if this does not sound like a libretto:

> O: There's the Drella. [*gasps*] It isn't, it isn't, it is! Ah!
> Drella! I know!
> ES: [*laughs*]
> AL: Who is Drella?
> O: You'll never get it from my lips, you filthy cod.
> ES: [*laughs*]
> O: I swear secrecy, Drella.
> ES: Sworn secrecy, Drella.
> DD: Who is Drella? What is Drella?

Drella, of course, was the Factory's name for Warhol (Dracula crossed with Cinderella) and after some long stretches of recitativo among the various characters, he intervenes and leads into one of the main themes by instructing Arthur to walk. Then Ondine picks it up:

Edie in her apartment with Donald Lyons, Dorothy Dean,
Ondine, and Arthur Loeb, in Andy Warhol, *Afternoon*, 1965
(16 mm film, black and white, sound, 100 minutes)

O: Walk to them  . . .

AW: Walk to us.

O: Walk to the camera, come on, love. Yeah.

AW: Walk for us.

AL: I thought making fun of cripples went out with Ben
Turpin.

Finally, Andy tells Ondine to make him walk, and Ondine comes in fortissimo: "Move. Limp over there, Arthur. Fall down, Rigoletto. Now move."

Now, if you never saw him, one conspicuous thing about Arthur Loeb, apart from his intelligence, was that he was quite crippled on his right side, which I always heard was due to an injury suffered in the womb. Throughout the film, his lameness is a recurring theme and the sadistic behavior of the others provides a lot of the action. So when there's a lapse, Ondine and Dorothy intervene with insults and lines like "Pinch him. Pinch him." Arthur says he can't feel anything on that side, and Dorothy says: "You don't feel anything anywhere, do you?" To all this Arthur responds quite lyrically but in a key of self-deprecation (once he even says, "I'm not defective, I'm retarded"), and clever Ondine sings opera buffa in counterpoint.

There are various secondary themes, such as the famous camp motif, which Andy introduces by telling Ondine to camp it up, to which Edie responds, "Oh, camp it up yourself," and Andy tells *her* to camp it up. However, there is another minor theme to do with Edie that I find really interesting, and that is her ignorance. How on earth does she manage in this highly sophisticated and verbal company? For one thing, when something gets her attention you see her trying to catch on. Thus when Arthur mentions Ben Turpin, she immediately wants to know who that is. At another point, Arthur asks, "What distinguishes us from the Greeks?" and she starts out teasing, "Pretending we're not bored?," but when he answers that the Greeks didn't even have a word for boredom, she's eager to know if that's true: "You're kidding. They did not have a word?" But the most telling exchange occurs when Ondine declares that he himself is not an arsonist but he has a friend called Tally who set his mother on fire, and that prompts Edie to say she doesn't like Joan of Arc. "Too martyr-ey," she says. Donald Lyons interjects that Joan was killed for refusing to wear women's clothes, and now Edie says, "You mean that's an historical fact?" Then she gets suspicious and accuses him of making fun of her ignorance. She *is* ignorant, but does it really make any difference? Clearly not, because now she states that Joan of Arc was killed for believing in witches, and the others pretty much let it go. So Edie holds her own somehow, and to give her credit, she has clearly been picking stuff up, because when she hears Donald mention Brasilia she says, "Brasilia. Oh do you know they've taken over a new government there?" And when somebody says the Kennedy brothers didn't expect LBJ to accept the vice presidency, to my great astonishment Edie says quite offhandedly, "That's Arthur Schlesinger." She also knows what she thinks of LBJ, which is not much.

Edie's main aria comes after Chuck Wein prompts her to tell everybody about her space theory, which she says will take hours, but she has some cameo moments as well, for instance when Dorothy says she should marry Karim (that's the young Aga Khan, whom I guess they had all known in Cambridge), and Edie tells about the time she tried to look him

up in Paris. She describes walking through the streets in a leotard and tights with a girl named Rosie in a rag dress down to
the ground and when they get to the house the butler comes
out and takes them for beggars. Ondine has some cameo moments too, apart from his duet with Arthur, but all his solos
are about getting drugs, first out of the car and then through
endless attempts to reach the dealer they call Rotten Rita or
the Mayor. This occupies a lot of reel three, and toward the
end of the reel Ondine can't wait another minute. He gets up
to leave, saying he'll give Edie a dosage and she must stick to
what he gives her. He tells her, "Forty minutes before you see
the man . . . take one quarter of it in a little piece of tissue.
Make a little . . ." And that's the last line of the film. It just
ends there, and I am left completely appalled and bewildered
by the treatment of Arthur Loeb. Just listen to how they taunt
him: Ondine says, "Whenever I see a Jew I see red," and Dorothy tells Arthur he's sick sick sick, "You are always sick. You
know, you are so boring because you're so sick sick sick."

What on earth is Warhol up to here? This is not just another example of his practice of throwing actors off balance,
putting the screws on them to make them reveal themselves,
because Arthur is entirely cool through it all. He parries all the
barbs and insults with perfect poise, even invites and abets
them, so he must have known what was coming and he's acting his part knowingly. There's nothing spontaneous about
it. In that case, the screws are on me, the audience, and I am
shocked by Andy's transgressiveness. Come to think of it,
both he and Edie were highly transgressive—they had that in
common, but with her it was instinctive; she just would not
recognize limits of any kind. With him, my sense is that it was

intentional and highly focused. I even think it was intelligent. There's one final thing about *Afternoon*: it makes me sad, because the third reel would have been the opening segment of *Chelsea Girls*, the most successful of all Warhol's movies, only Edie had it taken out. She refused to let it be included, because she was under contract to Bob Dylan's agent Al Grossman, and she had gotten it into her head that she was on her way to Hollywood.

Edie had been spending time with Bob Dylan right along, going to parties with him, visiting him at Grossman's place in Woodstock, and Dylan really got under Andy's skin. There were other reasons, but the main one was that he heard Dylan was going around blaming him for Edie taking drugs. Dylan had his own druggy world, only in his case, from what I read, the drug was heroin, whereas at the Factory it was always amphetamines, or speed. Andy took it in the form of a prescription diet pill called Obetrol, which he had begun taking in order to lose weight and now used to get himself jumped-up enough to be able to work fifteen hours a day and do without sleep. The truth is that Andy didn't do that to Edie; nobody did—she came that way. Perfectly legal drugs had been a fixture in her life since the time on the ranch when our father called the doctor in to shoot her full of tranquilizers and they kept her drugged and in bed for I don't know how long. And don't forget what they gave her in the psychiatric institutions, not to mention what her doctor was prescribing now. No one knew that side of Edie better than Ondine, who told Victor Bockris, "She was a non-stop drug addict period. And Andy didn't force her to take drugs . . . She was on drugs long before I ever met her. She had pharmacists. One of my jobs as her

French maid was to go to the pharmacist and get her uppers and downers and betweeners . . ."

By July the weather had turned warm, and Ondine was living in Central Park. He didn't need much money, he said, just enough to buy amphetamines, so when Edie mentioned that she needed a maid, he offered his services, and that's how he became Edie's French maid at a salary of thirty dollars a week. He'd get up in the morning, bathe in the lake, and head for Rotten Rita's place on the West Side, where he would get his amphetamines and while away the morning listening to opera until it was time to get Edie up. Then he would walk back across the park to her place on East Sixty-Third Street and begin the process of rousing her. It was not easy because of all the barbiturates she took, but he would give her a little amphetamine and that helped. Then he would put on opera records and make her breakfast, and eventually she would come to life and they would talk while she did her exercises, or he would put on her big dangly earrings and they would consult the I Ching, and all the time the phone would ring and ring and ring. Ondine was really more of a companion than a maid because Edie already had someone to do the cleaning, and besides, there was nobody in the world more companionable than Ondine. The arrangement lasted all summer and into the fall.

Meanwhile, Edie's fame had been building and she was getting more and more attention: in the mainstream press for her social persona as the beautiful young blue-blooded heiress who was said to have blown through a six-figure inheritance in a matter of months, in the Pop Art and underground film worlds for her association with Warhol and her superstardom, and in the fashion world for the novelty of her look. For Edie, with her cropped silver hair and tiny breasts and her bony athletic body, was truly androgynous. Remember, Twiggy didn't come on the scene until the following year, so this was quite a new type for a public accustomed to goddesses, whether soft, voluptuous Marilyn or those stark, unattainable figures in static poses and extreme attire that Richard Avedon and Irving Penn were photographing for *Vogue*. Instead, Edie was a scamp, and totally kinetic. She would run, leap, and turn cartwheels; she would balance on a ledge or dance in the surf, all the time making a performance out of just being herself. So now *Vogue* took note of her and included her in the famous "Youthquakers" piece in their August issue, where she appears in a leotard and tights, balancing spread-eagled on one foot on the back of her leather rhinoceros from Abercrombie's, the thing she called Wallow. The caption describes her as the star of Andy Warhol's underground movies and reports that "in Paris Warhol's gang startled the dancers at Chez Castel by appearing with fifteen rabbits and Edie Sedgwick in black leotard and a white mink coat." In fact, Edie gets the biggest illustration and one of the longest captions of anyone on the list, and consider who some of the other Youthquakers were: Peter Serkin, Joan Rivers, Frank Stella, and Bill Cosby, all in their twenties then, all just starting out, and all of them already highly accomplished.

So when it comes down to it, what was it about Edie, really?

Patti Smith really responded to that "Youthquakers" picture, and what she said about it was: "[Edie] was such a strong image that I thought, 'That's it.' It represented everything to

Edie modeling a dress by Betsey Johnson

Edie as Youthquaker, *Vogue*, August 1965 (Photograph by Enzo Sellerio)

me . . . radiating intelligence, speed, being connected to the moment." The image captured Patti's imagination so powerfully, she said, that she actually got a crush on Edie and would travel all the way to Manhattan just to hang around outside the discotheques that Edie frequented in hopes of catching a glimpse of her. And here's how she explained it: "You have to understand where I came from. Living in South Jersey, you get connected with the pulse beat of what's going on through what you read in magazines. Not even through records . . . I never saw people. I never went to a concert. It was all image." There you have it: *It was all image.*

Patti was in her late teens then, but Nora Ephron was older and she was annoyed. She wrote: "Edie Sedgwick is the girl that everybody is talking about. Nobody is quite sure who the everybody is who is talking about her, but no matter. There is too little now that is happening and too many words to write and television talk shows to film to leave a phenomenon like Edie Sedgwick alone." So there's an old sensibility that doesn't understand how someone with no accomplishments whatever can be getting all that attention, and there's a brand-new sensibility that's attuned only to images.

I'm reminded of something Andy said he realized as he was crossing the country in the summer of 1963, when he and Gerard were on their way to LA for his second show at the Ferus Gallery. The car belonged to the painter Wynn Chamberlain, who was driving, and the elfin underground film star Taylor Mead was along for the ride. Mead said Andy was scared to fly, but Andy claimed that he wanted to see what America looked like. Now, I too drove across the country in those years, and what I saw was the vast and changing landscape. Beyond that,

I saw what I chose to look at: courthouses in the South, pueblos and cliff dwellings in the Southwest, and the work of Frank Lloyd Wright wherever I could get to it. But what Andy saw was of a different order. He was looking at what was along the highway, and the farther west they went, the more Pop it all looked to him. As he put it, "Once you 'got' Pop, you could never see a sign the same way again. And once you thought Pop, you could never see America the same way again." Then he said this: "We were seeing the future and we knew it for sure. We saw people walking around in it without knowing it, because they were still thinking in the past, in the references of the past. But all you had to do was *know* you were in the future, and that's what put you there." Exactly: Andy recognized that the people he was seeing were living and perceiving everything in terms of the past, which was coming to an end without their knowing, while he and his friends were living in the future and they knew it. Patti Smith was so young she didn't even have to know it, she was simply living it. That's the divide between her and Nora Ephron. What Patti said about Edie signified something totally new, the existence of a public for whom it was all image. This was the future that Andy not only lived in but consciously embodied and exploited.

Andy's joy in looking may have been innate, but it must have been the illness that struck him in the fall of 1936 that taught him the intense pleasure of watching from a remove. When he was eight years old, he came down with Sydenham chorea, or St. Vitus dance, which is a disease you get when scarlet fever develops into rheumatic fever and then becomes a neurological disorder. It seems no one paid attention at first, and anyway, the family couldn't easily afford to take him to the doctor when his hands shook so he could hardly write, his feet dragged, and his speech became increasingly slurred. The other boys at school responded as boys will, by making fun of him and beating him up, so by the time the family was forced to take his condition seriously, he was terrified of school and shrank from social encounters. At first this applied only to other kids, but then a neighbor physically picked him off the ground and dragged him back to school by the shoulders, and after that it was everybody. So it must have been heaven for Andy to find himself confined to bed for months on end, with his doting and highly inventive mother plying him with comic books, paper dolls to cut out, books to color and supplies to color them with, and best of all, piles and piles of movie magazines. Nobody nowadays can possibly imagine what movies were in the thirties, or the sheer thrilling glamour of the stars, when ordinary life was so hard and drab and radio was all there was. No wonder that little boy was spellbound. A whole glorious world of glamorous celebrity opened up in his imagination, and he found he could actually approach it by, for instance, writing away for a picture of Shirley Temple, and possess it by cutting out images and forming collections of memorabilia. He got better, but then he had a relapse, and that meant several more months in bed, which is when those reddish blotches he had all his life began appearing all over his face and body. What I'd like to know is whether at the same time his whole body didn't become unusually sensitive, because one thing people say about him as an adult is that he really didn't like to be touched. Viva, one of the later superstars in the Factory, said that "if you so much as tried to touch Andy, he would actually shrink away . . .

I mean shrink backwards and whine . . . Any touch was like a burning poker." Gerard told Victor Bockris that Andy cringed from physical contact and that his shyness allowed him to be private, which indicates that he kept himself at a remove both physically and emotionally. And Andy's longtime friend Charles Henri Ford described him in the same terms: he said Andy didn't like to have anybody touch him or muss his hair, and that he preferred to be emotionless. Plus, of course, Andy himself told Gretchen Berg that he wanted to be like a machine. Only a person whose feelings and responses were excruciatingly acute would say something like that. Whatever the causes of his hypersensitivity, even if it was purely emotional, it's clear that when he grew up he preferred to hold back and shield himself, looking intensely but always from a certain distance, observing everything he wanted to observe, and allowing only his voracious inquisitiveness to engage directly. From what I understand, Andy rarely displayed any feeling, and when he was angry he would manifest it silently and indirectly for days on end. On the surface he was vague and noncommittal, always asking other people's opinions and never revealing his own, instead saying, "Oh, you think so? That's great," and maintaining that distance, that buffer zone between him and everything else out there.

Aside from the protection Andy gained from it, watching from a remove created a space for his perceptions, and at the same time, it slowed them down by postponing the moment of response, all of which had implications for his art. You have only to look at all the distancing strategies he adopted in producing his paintings. And as for his films, it wouldn't surprise me if it was that temporal lag (along with his love for the languorous look of old movies) that prompted him intuitively to show his early films several frames per second more slowly than they were shot. Here's how radical the effect was: Jonas Mekas reports that when Stan Brakhage saw *Sleep* at twenty-four frames per second, he was enraged by it, and when he watched it again at sixteen frames per second "an entirely new vision of the world stood clear before his eyes." Of course, in the case of the films that Andy made with Edie, it was her constant shifting responses he wanted to capture, so there was no reason to slow the film down, and now he was making one film after another with her, every one of them a critical success.

On the face of it, he and Edie seemed like a perfect fit. They both wanted almost exactly the same thing: Edie wanted people to notice her and accompany her and demand nothing in return, and Andy wanted to observe her and accompany her and he wanted nothing in return. Nothing, that is, except to film her, and that was one source of friction, because she never trusted the results. She needed to be sure she was doing something real, and she never could see how very real she was in Andy's films. Another complaint she had was that she couldn't get close to him, although they *were* close in so many ways—couldn't she sense the symbiosis between them? I think he identified with her, he would have liked to *be* her, to be a beautiful, glamorous girl who was the center of attention wherever she went. But he kept to himself inside his personal space, so she grew increasingly restless over time, and despite the fact that they were still seeing each other every day, going out together every night, and talking endlessly on the phone in between, she began to take her own distance and to rely more on Ondine for companionship.

Somebody once asked Ondine how he met Andy, and his response will tell you something about that watchful presence of Andy's. Ondine says he didn't actually meet him; he had gone to an orgy to have a good time and there was "this great presence at the back of the room. And this orgy was run by a friend of mine, and, so I said to this person, 'Would you please mind throwing that thing out of here?' And that thing was thrown out of there, and when he came up to me the next time, he said to me, 'Nobody has ever thrown me out of a party  . . .  Don't you know who I am?' And I said, 'Well, I don't give a good flying fuck who you are. You just weren't there. You weren't involved'  . . .  I wanted to be involved in some kind of orgy. This was the one thing that *I didn't understand* in the back of the room: it was Andy." Now, you might think he's saying that Andy was a voyeur, but that's not where Ondine's going. Instead, he says, "[A]nd from that point on we became *really good friends*  . . .  And he understood that I understood that he understood  . . .  He's a very feeling, a very caring, a very *human* person." Here Ondine's point is that in the midst of the orgy he had sensed that powerful watchful presence and was disturbed because he didn't understand it; the minute he and Andy understood each other he could see what a good person Andy was and they became really good friends. Still, there are those, like Truman Capote, and even Henry Geldzahler, who did call Andy a voyeur, and I think "spectator" would be a better word, because to most people "voyeur" implies someone who gets satisfaction out of looking at sex organs and observing sex acts, and while he certainly did all of that and he had a huge collection of pornography, that's not the whole picture of what Andy was up to. To begin with, conscious, deliberate observation is a fundamental part of being a visual artist, and he was acutely visual even for an artist. Second, I think watching avidly at a remove was his way of being in the world, and watching people engage in every kind of sexual behavior was just one part of the whole spectrum of looking and seeing whatever interested him, every minute detail of every single thing. Moreover, it wasn't just looking and seeing; he also wanted to hear everything and capture what he heard, and for that he had what he called his wife, which was the cassette tape recorder that he carried with him everywhere he went.

In Andy's hands, that tape recorder could be just as relentless as the lens; for instance, during the taping of *a: a novel*, he was so intent on capturing everything Ondine said and did that he even pursued him into the lavatory when he was frantic to be alone on the toilet. The book grew out of Gerard Malanga's suggestion that if Andy really wanted to produce a book, he should make a novel out of a series of cassette tapes. Andy loved the idea, because he did want to write a book— it was part of his campaign to branch out into every major medium—only he was hopelessly incapable of writing. So he decided to tape a day in the life of Ondine, and they arranged to start at Fifth Avenue and Eighty-Sixth Street at 2:00 p.m. on Friday, July 30. Andy got there a bit late, bringing his tape recorder and twelve cassettes, each containing an hour's worth of tape, plus enough Obetrols of various strengths to guarantee that Ondine would stay awake and lively for the next twelve hours even though he had been high for days and hadn't slept at all. Andy gives him six blue ones to get started, and they set off toward Madison Avenue, gossiping as they go. So begins this postmodern picaresque novel, and those first twelve tapes go on for nearly three hundred pages, during which Ondine, with his delirious loquacity and total lack of inhibition, proves to be a perfect protagonist. For my purposes, however, the book is interesting because Edie figures in a large part of it, and you can get a sense of her immediate presence and the way she talked. Then when she's not present, you can hear how the others talk about her.

The story is simple: the two of them wander down Madison as far as Seventy-Seventh Street, where they duck into Stark's for juice and pastry and Andy spots Robert Rauschenberg, who doesn't notice him. Andy gives Ondine five orange Obetrols, and they take a cab to the Factory, where they're expecting a delivery. The package arrives, and it's the EL.8015/II model videotape camera that Philips Norelco is lending Andy for a month in hopes of publicity. (That's what Andy says, anyway, but I see Callie Angell says it was *Tape Recording Magazine* that lent it to him in exchange for an exclusive interview.) Then comes the toilet episode, in which Andy gets his way and Stephen Shore documents it, and eventually Edie and Chuck appear and after a bit they go off with Ondine and Andy to Lester Persky's place so Ondine can have a bath in Persky's rust-free tub. After the bath they go out on the terrace and Ondine and Edie talk and talk, until their French friend Genevieve Charbin arrives, and they go look for a place to get something to eat. They drop Edie off at home, Ondine walks her up the stairs and tells her to try not to take any Nembutals and to get some sleep, then he and the others go on to Rotten

Rita's place on the Upper West Side, where Rotten gives everybody a shot of amphetamines one at a time in the bathroom. Meanwhile, who should call but the Duchess (i.e., Brigid Berlin), who's in Roosevelt Hospital for observation, and everybody can hear her because she's on speakerphone, and she tells them about all the stuff she's managing to steal. And so it goes, until finally they leave and take a cab downtown, dispersing along the way, and as tape number twelve runs out, Andy tells Ondine to say his last words. Ondine says his last words are "Andy Warhol," and they say goodbye. In the end, that was all the taping they did, so when they got round to publishing the book, which was not until 1967, they had to make up the other twelve hours out of miscellaneous tapes they had lying around.

As I said, you can learn quite a lot about Edie, how the others respond to her, and what she's like around them. Her name in the Factory was Taxi, but in the book they call her Taxine, Andy is Drella, and Ondine, of course, is Ondine. So he and Drella have not walked very far when Ondine remarks that it's awful working for Taxine, you can't support yourself, but, he says, she has some TV appearances coming up and he's told her how to handle herself. Drella asks what Ondine thinks of her, and Ondine answers that they're not having sex, no matter what people believe. Drella tells him people are saying he's fucking her up with drugs, and Ondine says he just asks if she wants a drug and if she wants it she takes it, but she does have a problem, uh, slipping barbiturates; she takes too many of her sleeping pills and needs to cut down. They get to the Factory, and while they wait around for the delivery man, Ondine mentions that the Duchess has been a drug fiend since she was twelve, and Drella says Taxine has been drugged too and she's young. Then Drella tells Ondine Taxine adores him, but Ondine brushes that aside and explains that she desperately wants to believe in what she's doing and perhaps doesn't quite believe it as much as she says. He also mentions that she lies a lot. Drella says that's great and now he asks if she's a nymphomaniac. (Hang on! Andy and Edie have been inseparable since the end of March, the two of them are the most famous couple in town, and he has to ask Ondine a question like that? But then I realize, of course, Andy loved listening to gossip almost as much as he liked watching; he just wants to get Ondine going about Edie.) Ondine answers that she indulges her passions and hates herself for it. He adds that she's always telling him his mother is the best, whereas her family hates her because she's so great that she's just hated by everybody. The conversation then shifts to Ondine's old grandmother who's taken to going about in his dead grandfather's trousers, and the two of them ramble on about this and that until suddenly Edie comes in, and just listen to them, how excited they are:

[ONDINE:] Oh, Bonjourno! Oh.
[DRELLA:] Oh the movie's here, the camera. No, how was your, our day? Hey, . . . I'm following Ondine today, Taxi. (*Ondine sings.*) Taxi I'm following Ondine today.

Ondine offers to play a Callas album, and Edie says she might go right out of her mind. What she wants instead is to tell them that because of her cold she got her money and spent a thousand dollars and now she has thirty-five dollars to live on for the next month, and what happened to her today, which is this:

> (T) People came to the door saying they had checks from like two weeks ago that were bouncing and that I've written three checks since then ohhhhhhhhhh! And so I, I called mummy and I said "You, I'm doing this because uh I'm trying to say what I really think and believe and and you've twisted me basically ever since I was born and I've made mistakes but I've you know I've done it in a way that was genuinely Micky [*sic*] and I fe—and I'm doing it now in in a much more wide open space and I and the reason for the publicity is to avoid being squashed out by people that use you like dirt."

So far, Edie's lucid enough. In the cab on the way to Persky's place, she and Chuck describe their experiences with Merv Griffin's people preparing for the show, and when they arrive Ondine takes his bath. Afterward they go out on the terrace and talk. Edie starts out okay. She says the police are after her; she left her car in a bus stop on Fifth Avenue for two days, Ondine says he noticed it, and she tells him all about the cop questioning her about it. Then when they're alone, she gets going on the subject of people not understanding, and talks on and on about how she's trying to get people to understand things they'll never understand, until she suddenly pauses and asks, "Why do I keep hanging on about Drella?" Ondine tells her it's because she's so young, and she says that's true and goes back to saying people have to learn and she knows it and she's right. Eventually, she winds up in the stratosphere and Ondine's right up there with her, the two of them playing some kind of game involving gradations of stardom:

> o—Divinity star, third, what's the next category? After a star is what. Has-been . . .
> T—Something that's that's um, what's next to a star that's . . . No no no, this is closer to divinity is
> . . .
> o—After star, would that be fledging?
> T—No no no, gone down from divinity to star to somehow the mockery walks get in, but they get out of it by bottles.

And by the end of it she's talking like this:

> T—And spit and sh, y'know, shit, spit, and schlitz . . .
> [o] That's right my dear.
> T—which is split as well as the monger is somebody who, who's yeah grabby grabby which is worse than penny pigging. A schlitz would be you know, would be worse than a peeny pig.

And so on . . . What I want to know is, how on earth did she manage like that? And yet she did, she kept going, and there was a whole lot more ahead for her, including Girl of the Year. The taping took place on July 30, the day the Norelco videotape camera arrived, and now Andy took that camera and used it to make *Outer and Inner Space*.

Early in July, he had made another film in the series representing twenty-four hours in the life of Edie Sedgwick. It
was called *Beauty #2*, and I have to confess, all I could see in it
was Edie and a boy called Gino Piserchio in their underwear,
rolling around rather unconvincingly on a daybed with a dog
nearby and a man (Chuck Wein) off camera saying things to
get Edie upset. I know it's my failure, because Jonas Mekas really admired the film and Stephen Koch, for whom I have the
utmost respect, called it "an almost ideal example of Warhol's
technique of the period and one of the stronger films from
any period of his career." Never mind—I do understand what
Koch means when he says what he saw in Edie on-screen. The
qualities he points out—that "she never played the female
clown," "she always kept her cool," "when she spoke she made
sense, her response to a contretemps on screen . . . was
never the customary hysteria, but a visibly intelligent effort
to cope," and that "[i]n *Kitchen* . . . [she] is noticeable as
a grown-up woman, good-naturedly playing along with the
joke"—all seem to me to reflect the perception that she was always completely her own self. He virtually says so: "[She] glows
with absolutely self-absorbed narcissism . . . But there was
something else . . . , a certain unshakeable attention to the
real, a certain belief in the truths of her presence as a woman."
Gerard Malanga said much the same thing: he described her
"vivid and penetrating eyes, full of small timidities, which recorded perhaps the shock that too great an honesty expects
from life," and went on to say, "When she spoke she made
sense. She could not be the fool or be made to look foolish."
What tributes those are, and I think that what both Koch and

Malanga were responding to in Edie was precisely what made her so good for Andy's purposes, namely, that she was entirely and genuinely herself at all times. He told Gretchen Berg, "I leave the camera running until it runs out of film because that way I can catch people being themselves . . . You get a better picture of people [when they're] being themselves instead of trying to act like they're themselves." That's the thing about Edie, she was completely incapable of being anything *but* herself; it's all she was interested in, being herself freely. So Andy was able both to use her and to depict her exactly as she was, and that included her self-doubt.

Edie's response to herself is the subject of *Outer and Inner Space*; that was clear from what I saw in the museum at Andover, but then I couldn't hear the sound. Since then I have seen a transcript of the soundtrack, and Edie's self-doubt runs all through it, starting with her first words. Her image on the television monitor says, "[B]etween positive and negative . . . it's the simplest definition I can think of," and the "real" Edie winces and says, "Ohhhh. I can't stand it. I refuse to listen to it. I can't stand it. It's stupid. It's stupid . . . have to stop it," and she screams. A little later, her image says, "No emotional qualities are ever attached to it . . . no specific individual concerns and from that point of view . . . and individual perspective because the minute you take the time to pay attention to one specific thing you're denying the time to . . . other specific things . . . and what it is you are . . . it's happening all the time . . . choosing what to notice and what not to notice . . . and what is in line with your own developmental growth"; and the "real" Edie responds with contempt, "It sounds like a lot of bullshit—it does. You don't think so? D-R-A-G." And further on she says, "[I]t makes me so nervous to have to listen to it. It really is rotten, but it's so pathetic. I never dreamt I was so pathetic." Her response is excruciating, but in the end the soundtrack turned out to be incidental, because what Andy did was this: he made the videotape, then he made two thirty-three-minute sound reels of Edie reacting to her video image, and then he redoubled the whole thing by projecting the two reels on two screens side by side, so that all four faces of Edie were talking and what they said was almost completely unintelligible. All I can say is, I would give anything to have seen that quadruple portrait; the little that I did see was so extraordinary.

Remember, there was no such thing as video art, Nam June Paik didn't even own a camera, when Andy Warhol made this film. To give you an idea of its originality and sheer brilliance, as well as its connection to his paintings, it is worth quoting from Callie Angell's lucid account: "In this film . . . Warhol can be seen reworking certain formal and aesthetic concerns—with media, multiple imagery, celebrity, and portraiture—which he previously explored in depth in his serial silk-screen portraits of movie stars of the early sixties . . . [T]he emotional fractures which are apparent in Edie Sedgwick's performance—and which are, in many ways, the real topic of this film—articulate the metaphysical and psychological difficulties of portraiture with a specificity that is only hinted at in Warhol's paintings . . . The 'outer and inner space' of Warhol's title delineates the metaphysical confrontation established by this scenario: on the left, a brightly glowing video image transforms Sedgwick's profile into a flattened glamorized mask which seems almost vapid in its graphic simplicity, on the right the filmed face of the 'real' Edie, shadowed and expressively modeled by the glow of her own video image, exposes every detail of her increasingly unhappy subjectivity as she endures the ordeal of this face-off with her televised self. 'Outer and inner,' therefore, refers not only to the dichotomy between Sedgwick's outer beauty and inner turmoil, so vividly diagrammed in this double portrait, but it also describes the two very different spaces of representation occupied by the video/television medium and by film."

Then she writes, "In the context, it is significant that Sedgwick seems to be unnerved, not by the film camera she is facing, but by the uncanny presence of her own prerecorded image looking over her shoulder from the television behind her. Video—and perhaps television as well—seems to be directly implicated as the instrument of her suffering . . . Sedgwick's distress, in the end, emerges as the direct product of the act of portraiture: the tension that arises between the living reality of a person and the image that person is reduced to, a conflict which she must literally act out, in real time, in this film."

But if you listen carefully, what Edie finds distressing here is her living reality. It's hearing herself, realizing that what she tries so hard to communicate, the truth she's always talking about that she is so desperate to have everyone understand, is completely incoherent. What the soundtrack so devastatingly reveals is her inner chaos and her response as she is confronted with it. And when you have seen the film, you see Edie differently: you realize that what you saw publicly was all surface and energy; only here do you see what went on inside.

To me, *Outer and Inner Space* is a very great work of art, and it kills me that Edie had no idea what it meant to be its

Andy Warhol, *Outer and Inner Space*, 1965 (16 mm film, black and white, sound, 66 minutes or 33 minutes in double screen)

subject. She simply couldn't understand; she was always worried about looking ridiculous. At this point, Edie's doubts were becoming a problem. People in Dylan's circle were telling her she was wasting herself, that she could be the next great Hollywood star, and Andy, who had his own eye on Hollywood (which in my opinion shows he was just as naïve as she was), would try to explain that the more she appeared in his films, the more likely it was that she would be seen and picked up by an agent. But Edie didn't believe it, and she kept haranguing him with her doubts, which must be why she wasn't included in their next film. It was called *My Hustler*, and from the outset it was entirely Chuck Wein's project. He claimed that he told Edie about it at a party and she said she wasn't interested; but Bockris says Chuck was making a move because he saw her position slipping. Whatever the reason, they carried on with the planning, and when Labor Day came round and they were ready to film, they did it all without her.

Edie, meanwhile, was short of money for drugs and clothes, so she was imposing on her friends. Brigid Berlin's sister Richie says Edie would appear at her door wanting a bath and a poke and a tuna sandwich from the drugstore downstairs, then she'd ask if Richie had anything she could wear. Meanwhile, the phone would be ringing the whole time—people looking for Edie. The two of them would outfit themselves in Richie's designer clothes, and when Edie was all poked up and looking fantastic out they would go shoplifting, starting, for example, at Lord & Taylor. Richie said it was like Broadway: "You'd go in and you're up for the Academy Awards on the ground floor . . . There was nothing to make you feel marvelous like a quick purchase. Bath products. A little of this, a little of that. Edie didn't care. She'd say, 'Listen, we'll go and get these fabulous things. We can trade them for cash.'" And Edie wasn't only shoplifting, she was stealing from her friends, drugs in particular. After she left they'd find that she had gotten into whatever they had, wherever they had it, and sometimes she would leave a charming little note saying *IOU*.

Genevieve Charbin was living with Edie at the time, and she describes how they would spend the day. First thing in the morning, she says, Edie would appear in her dirty negligée with her hair all mussed up, bringing breakfast and a pill so Genevieve would get up faster and start doing things for her, like buying her cases of makeup or going to the laundry. The two of them would discuss the night before and then they would get on the phone with Andy, who would tell them every little thing he had done from the second he woke up, and he (whose routine included a hundred pull-ups) would prescribe exercises for Edie. And when they weren't talking to Andy, there would be other calls, interviews, or men from the night before wanting to see Edie, in which case she would have to make excuses, because at night she never went out with anybody but Andy. Next she would spend literally hours making up her face, and when she was done it was always flawless and would stay that way through all the countless parties, right until the sun came up. Then in the late afternoon they would go down to the Factory, where it was always very busy, Genevieve said, and at night they would go to the parties.

Edie was at her most dazzling that summer, and one of the people she dazzled was the evening reporter for the *Journal American*, a nice man called Mel Juffe. He was covering a big party at the Scene on West Fortieth Street, where some of Andy and Edie's movies were being projected on the wall; they were there, and that's how Mel met them. He told Andy later, "When I was seeing you and Edie, you two were at your absolute pinnacle as a media couple. You were *the* sensation from about August through December of '65. Nobody could figure you out, nobody could even tell you apart—and yet no event of any importance could go on in this town unless both of you were there." Mel was so smitten with Edie that for the next few months he was around all the time. That's how it happened that she asked him to arbitrate between her and Andy one night at the Russian Tea Room when they met to discuss her career. Jonas Mekas had just offered Andy a series of nights at the Cinematheque, and Andy wanted to have an Edie Sedgwick retrospective; Edie, however, would have none of it. She claimed that Andy wanted to make a fool out of her, that everybody in New York was laughing at her, she was embarrassed to leave her apartment, and on and on like that. Furthermore, she thought she should be paid. She was talking that way a lot now, not only because she was desperate for cash but also because people were putting it into her head. Mel tried to tell her she was the envy of every girl in New York, which God knows she was, but she just went on insisting that the retrospective was one more way for them to make a fool out of her, until finally Andy got so upset he turned red in the face and could hardly speak. He told her, "But don't you *understand*? These movies are art!" (This is Andy's own account of the scene, and I find it interesting. First of all, I'm impressed that Andy, who always acted so very nonchalant and vague, would drop all his defenses and come out with such a statement; and second, I wonder what it means that he would put it all in writing all these years later, given how very private he was about his feelings. Also, there's the fact that Pat Hackett was the one putting his speech into written words, because the books published in Andy's name were all produced from tapes.) In the end, Andy walked out and Mel and Edie sat up all night talking until she reached some decision. But then as usual she changed her mind, and the next day they were all back to square one . . .

Andy said Edie kept vacillating "between enjoying the camp of making movies with us and worrying about her image, and by vacillate I mean she'd go back and forth from hour to hour. She could be standing, talking to a reporter, and she'd look over at us and giggle, then tell him something arch like 'I don't mind being a public fool—as long as I'm communicating myself and reaching people.'" That was a constant refrain with Edie; she was always saying she wanted to reach people and make them understand, but understand what? If you think about it, she *did* communicate herself, and very earnestly, in *Outer and Inner Space*, and you know what her response was to that. But now her resentment and mistrust were wearing on Andy, and at the same time, even Ondine thought she was taking way too many drugs. What with one thing and another, it was December before they made another movie with her, and then, all too appropriately, it was *Lupe*. (That's the one about the Hollywood star who planned to commit the perfect suicide, except the drugs made her vomit and she wound up dying with her head in the toilet. The film is in color, so what you see is Edie with peroxide-blond hair in a fancy bed with a wall of mirror doubling her as she puts on her makeup and chats with Billy Name, who's trimming her hair, and that's the preparation part. Then you see her dressed in a pale blue Empire gown with a green sash, drifting vaguely about a formal dining room, sitting down at the table, all the while getting more and more stoned—and it didn't look to me as if she was acting. And because Andy showed it on two screens simultaneously, at the end you got two long views of her lying there on the bathroom floor with her head hanging over the toilet.)

But all during that late summer she never stopped going to the Factory every day and out everywhere with Andy every night, and the whole time she kept going back and forth about being in Andy's films. She simply didn't understand, and remembering how Andy said if she'd needed a script she wouldn't have been right for *Poor Little Rich Girl*, I think if she had been capable of understanding what he was doing and how his work was being received, she would not have been right.

## SEPTEMBER-OCTOBER

In America, Labor Day is the invariable sign that summer is coming to an end, and in 1965 that weekend on Fire Island when they filmed *My Hustler* with Genevieve Charbin in place of Edie seems to have been a sign that the high season of Edie Sedgwick and Andy Warhol was coming to an end. The idea for the film was Chuck Wein's, and he and Dorothy Dean put it all together: the money, the location on Fire Island, even the cast, which consisted of Ed Hood, Genevieve Charbin, Dorothy herself, and her beloved Joe Campbell (alias the Sugar Plum Fairy), plus somebody called John McDermott and the new star Paul America, a gorgeous lost hunk Persky had picked up somewhere hitchhiking. In Andy's words, "It was the story of an old fag who brings a butch blond hustler out to Fire Island for the weekend and his neighbors all try to lure the hustler away," and all Andy did was shoot it. Actually, Chuck tried to take over that aspect of the project as well, because he was determined to use editing and a moving camera, and both were strictly against Andy's principles. So when they were all out there on Fire Island about to start filming, Chuck went to Paul Morrissey and Gerard and said, "We can't let Andy just turn the camera on and let it run—we're not going to waste this whole trip. You operate the camera, and I'll tell them what to do, and we'll make something like a real movie with stops and starts." Paul and Gerard wouldn't go along, but apparently that's not all there was to Chuck Wein's subversiveness. At dinner after the shooting, somebody laced the orange juice with Sandoz acid, which most accounts say hit Andy particularly hard because he had never taken LSD, and everybody said it was Chuck who did it. Bockris, however, reports that Andy was so afraid of such an eventuality that he had brought a supply of candy bars, intending to consume nothing but those and tap water all weekend. Both stories could be true.

Just as summer dawdles on to the equinox, Edie and Andy continued to go about together, and on September 13, they made one of their more spectacular appearances. Andy was invited to the New York Film Festival at Lincoln Center, where *The Vampires* was being shown; he came in a tuxedo, and Edie swept in at his side wearing a black leotard and tights and trailing a black ostrich-feather cape. That entrance got into all the papers. Somebody told me that at a certain point Edie got up and danced in the aisle, but I don't know if it's true. Sounds like her, though, doesn't it?

What was on Andy's mind at this moment, however, was not films but making a statement. In Steven Watson's words, he "wanted to create a work that eluded definition in the art world and at the same time memorialized the art career that he was ready to let drift away." And what would accomplish that more perfectly than a work of art that would float up to the sky? Already the year before, Andy had thought of making a floating light bulb, but his engineer friend Billy Klüver had told him it couldn't be done; now, however, Klüver told him about a material called Scotchpak, and Andy came up with a better idea. So on October 4, a small group gathered in the Factory—Andy and Gerard and Billy Klüver, plus Pontus Hultén, who happened to be in town working on the Stockholm retrospective—and made the first *Silver Cloud*, a narrow silver tube forty feet long with a conical head and a limp sleeve of a tail. They hauled it up to the roof, where they filled it with helium, Billy Name took pictures, and Andy let it go. The exhilaration as they watched it float up and away over the city must have been fantastic. Pontus Hultén remarked that it was the first work of art to be sent into space. Then when it was all over and they went back downstairs, the person Andy called was Genevieve Charbin. But of course, it was Edie who accompanied him to Philadelphia a few days later for the opening of the retrospective that brash young Sam Green was staging to inaugurate the Institute of Contemporary Art.

Samuel Adams Green was a huge and early admirer of Andy Warhol. They met in 1961, and in 1963, as a twenty-three-year-old gallery assistant at the Green Gallery in New York, Sam put on the first show ever of Pop Art, at Wesleyan University, where his father happened to be chairman of the art history department. Sam was well connected in Philadelphia as well, and had already taken Andy and a motley cohort to stay with his distant cousin, the distinguished patron and collector Henry McIlhenny, at his very grand and well-staffed house on Rittenhouse Square. (McIlhenny was the president of the Philadelphia Museum; he was elegant and fastidious, and while he had not the faintest interest in Andy's work, he was also gay and apparently got a big kick out of Andy himself and his outlandish friends.) Also through family connections, either directly (I read somewhere that he sent in his application under his father's official letterhead) or indirectly (he knew a number of the trustees), Sam got himself appointed director of exhibitions at the gallery that the University of Pennsylvania had just set up to expose students to contemporary art. He then persuaded the board to let him put on a retrospective of the work of Andy Warhol, and as he intended to make a very big splash with it, he had been priming the pump every way he knew how. It was the first time an art opening had been conceived and organized as a media event. Sam saw to it that Andy's movies were shown around town. He put up posters everywhere, even went so far as to have blouses made for the ladies of the board and a tie for himself out of silk cloth printed with S&H Green Stamps to match the posters. For a show of twenty-seven works of art installed in a couple of not-very-large rooms, he sent out at least four thousand invitations and contacted a bunch of television news stations and reporters from the print media, as well as everyone he knew in New York and every celebrity and art world person he could think of. Andy, for his part, brought a professional from New York with a two-turntable rig and speakers to provide the music. The rest is history.

Sam said he knew what was coming, but it seems Andy himself was completely unprepared. He and Edie and Gerard and Chuck and various others, including my old friend Ken Lane, were all staying with Henry McIlhenny, and on opening night they went to dinner with the president of the board, Mrs. Gates Lloyd, out on the Main Line. That's how it happened that Edie and Andy didn't arrive at the gallery until twenty to ten, by which time the music was blaring and there were at least a thousand people, including every element that Sam had invited, from students and trustees to all kinds of celebrities and out-of-towners—even seventeen-year-old Patti Smith found out about it and came—all jammed into a space that might have held four hundred comfortably.

Here's Andy's own description of what happened:

When we walked into the Philadelphia opening there were floodlights turned on us and television cameras. It was very hot and I was all in black—T-shirt, jeans, short jacket, what I always wore in those days—and the yellow-lens wraparound sun/ski glasses didn't keep the glare out; I wasn't ready for it. There were four thousand kids packed into two rooms. They'd had to take all my paintings . . . off the walls because they were getting crushed. It was fabulous: an art opening with no art! . . . The music was going full blast and all the kids were doing the jerk . . .

When the kids saw me and Edie walk in, they started actually screaming. I couldn't believe it . . . They had to lead us through the crowd—the only place we wouldn't get mobbed was on some iron stairs that led up to a sealed-off door. They put guards at the bottom of the steps so nobody would rush us. All the people we came down with from New York were on those steps . . . , and Sam too. Edie was wearing a pink floor-length T-shirt dress made out of stretchy Lurex-type material.

Opening of the Andy Warhol retrospective at the Institute of
Contemporary Art, Philadelphia, October 8, 1965

It had elastic sleeves that were supposed to stay rolled up but she unrolled one of them about twelve feet past her arm—perfect . . . because she could have a drink in one hand and be draping and dipping and dangling her sleeve over the heads of the crowd below. She was putting on the performance of her life.

And so she was. Andy just stood there, white-faced, and watched—some say he was terrified, others say he was enraptured by Edie—as somebody handed her a microphone and she began to play the crowd. She welcomed them, she charmed them, she kept searching among them for someone she knew, and she was glad to sign Andy's name to whatever was passed up to her. And all the time she was dangling that sleeve, playing Rapunzel in the fairy tale, letting down her golden hair to an adoring public. This went on for two whole hours until finally a graduate student appeared with a crowbar and hacked through the blocked door at the top of the stairs, and she and Andy were able to escape.

It was the night of October 8, 1965, and unbeknownst to Edie herself or to those present—not even Andy could have sensed it—this was the zenith, the absolute high point of her life and the apotheosis of Edie Sedgwick. Now, as she passed through that opening with Andy, her image detached itself from her person, and while her person went across the roof and down to a waiting police car, and gradually at first but then faster and faster downhill from there, her image rose and floated away over the city. After a time you could see it from any point in the world.

# NOTES FOR MY
# DEAD BROTHER

My brother Bobby

*Bobby, I had assumed all along that if I just laid out the evidence, if I considered the personal and social circumstances of our family and how things changed over time, if I reconstructed as best I could our sister Edie's life and what went on during the months when she was with Andy Warhol, if I did all this I might be able to answer the questions I put to you in my mind when I saw what was happening. Instead, certain things have become obvious, and many of my questions have turned out to be irrelevant. So now I have other questions, and beyond that, I have some ideas and some miscellaneous observations.*

One way of looking at the conjunction of Edie Sedgwick and Andy Warhol in 1965 would be to see it as a mythological event. Each of them was on a powerful trajectory, and when their trajectories intersected, a bright binary star suddenly appeared and dazzled the public. Edie had a particular combination of attributes and an indefinable inborn force that Andy was able to engage and put to use for both of them, and in the process he got a terrific enabling impetus from her, not just socially and personally but also as a filmmaker. But what he did for her was beyond measure. In any other circumstances, Edie would have been an ephemeral and purely local phenomenon—she flamed out so fast. Her arc was short, but his had a different angle of incidence, and he was going far. He would have made it into high society and the company of celebrities sooner or later no matter what, just not from such a distance, not in the same innocent frolicsome spirit as he did with Edie, and he would have made other innovative films, just not the ones he made with her. However, there was something about the two of them together—their particular symbiosis and combined insouciant daring—that alerted the public to something new. Andy embodied it, his attitude and understanding informed it, and Edie was its face. That's how her image came to be a real superstar, and why it's still up there, in some ways brighter than ever.

The gossip columns called her a debutante, an heiress, and a Boston Brahmin, but Edie was nothing of the sort. She was never a debutante—she just went to a few parties; she stood to inherit some money but hardly a fortune; and despite the presence of many Sedgwick relatives in Boston, neither side of her family came from there. The fact is, Edie came from California, from a privileged but troubled family living in isolation on a large cattle ranch, where for long stretches of time in adolescence she was completely isolated under the control of her parents; furthermore, she had spent nine months of her short life in mental hospitals. What formed her was life on the ranch, which was one of ambiguity and extremes: on the one hand the sheer exhilaration of physical existence, the seductive beauty and ease of the surface, and on the other the undercurrents of emotional violence, the tension arising from all that was denied and suppressed. Edie appeared to have been given everything, and materially that may have been so, but humanly she was deprived and incapacitated. So when she left the ranch for the larger world, she was not the magical innocent being she may have seemed, she was not Miranda in *The Tempest*, she was more like a feral creature springing out of captivity. You would never have seen her that way, however, because Edie was truly enchanting, and there was something about her that commanded attention and stirred up excitement wherever she went.

Thinking about her ascent, I always imagined that once Edie entered the liberating ambience of the Factory and came into her own she was free. But Chuck Wein, who knew her better than anyone in those years, said that wasn't true. Quite the opposite: all she could relate to was the family and the ranch. "[T]hat's where most of her experience was," he said, "plus fear of what might affect her reality . . . [N]othing that was happening in New York, no matter how interesting it was, or good for her, wiped that out. In other words, the idea that she had to worry about being locked up was more important than being in *Vogue*. She'd put her all into it, and she would do it, and she did it, and she just was herself in it, but she didn't care. It was still back there. What they could do to her. That was on her mind."

Of course Edie knew and feared what her parents could do to her reality; how could it be otherwise? They had established their control once and for all when she tried to tell the truth about Fuzzy and he called the doctor and declared her mentally ill. No wonder the Factory couldn't set Edie free. Nothing about it, not all the freedom and opportunity Andy gave her to express and realize herself, none of the stunning success, none of the fame was enough: all that time Edie was fleeing for her life, always looking back at the danger at her heels and abandoning herself to the danger ahead.

Edie didn't understand what had happened in Philadelphia, but Ondine did, and here's how he explained it to her: he said the reason people stood outside the museum chanting "Edie and Andy" was, they were "*that* relevant." Edie said it was like an insane response from a whole culture, and Ondine told her that's just what it was, all those people were relating to her for a very good reason. He told her she was the queen of the whole scene and to accept it: "If you're going to be that kind of culture hero, my *God*! Assume the mantle. Wear it! Be the culture hero."

So what exactly was it about Edie that made her a culture hero? What was the public responding to? Patti Smith said it: "She was such a strong image that I thought, 'That's it.'" What's striking here is that Patti Smith speaks of Edie not as having an image, but as *being* one. It's the image, not Edie, she's talking about when she says: "It represented everything to me . . . radiating intelligence, speed, being connected with the moment." Clearly, a shift has taken place from the real to the image, from depth and complexity to the surface, and it's no longer the image that's ephemeral; reality itself seems to have lost its substance. What I want to know is, now that the image has become something in its own right, what is it an image of?

But as Andy said, "[M]ore than anything people just want stars," and Edie's image became precisely the kind of superstar that she herself was so unsure about, which so easily might have been ridiculous if people had seen it that way. And in fact some did see it that way, including Nora Ephron, including me, but this new public didn't. Instead, they flocked to Edie because she represented what they were ready for, the era of the image, which was just coming into being. Andy anticipated it, although even he was unprepared for the epiphany in Philadelphia.

Patti Smith's description of the opening in Philadelphia makes it all very clear: "Edie was coming down this long staircase. I think she had ermine wrapped around her; her hair was white, and her eyebrows black. She had on this real little dress. I think she had these two . . . unless I dreamt it . . . big white afghan hounds on black leashes with diamond collars, but that could be fantasy." She's right, it is fantasy; and how is it that the reality wasn't striking enough to leave an impression? After all, there was Edie in her floor-length pink jersey Rudi Gernreich dress, standing for two hours halfway up that iron staircase with a drink in her hand, playing to the crowd and tantalizing them by dangling her unfurled sleeve over their heads. Why invent an ermine wrap and dogs in diamond collars?

But what Patti Smith saw was what she was looking for, a fantasy image of upper-class glamour, and she defended that: "People think it's superficial, but I thought and still do that my consciousness about it was great. I always thought that the world of the upper class was really fantastic."

At first I thought what Patti got from looking at Edie was

the same kind of romantic experience that I got from reading English novels about the upper classes. But Patti wasn't reading a story or even looking at pictures, she was looking at Edie *in person*, and what she saw was an image that accommodated her fantasy. It seems that memory, which clings to every least detail, is of little use to fantasy; all fantasy wants is the image to dwell on.

Edie and Andy's joint image was established when they appeared together at the Met opening. Simply by appearing, they became celebrities. Originally, the word signified an attribute: someone who was well known was a "person of celebrity." Now, however, celebrity means a person enjoying "fame and broad public recognition  . . . , as a result of the attention given to them by mass media."

So these days there's a whole agglomeration of celebrities known as the Kardashians. They are said to be America's most famous family, and according to the internet they achieved this status by parlaying a notorious 2002 sex tape into a reality TV show and a business empire. The difference between Edie and the Kardashians is that these people really know how to turn their celebrity into money. If Edie had known how to do that, she wouldn't have had to keep asking our parents.

I first heard the term "influencer" a couple of years ago when a friend of ours, a former diplomat who now lives in Madrid, happened to mention that his fourteen-year-old granddaughter Katia had just become one—she had been picked up on the street by a scout from a modeling agency—and her meteoric rise reminded him of Edie. I got in touch with our friend to ask about Katia, and I was completely dumbfounded by his response, because this is what he wrote:

Edie was a trendsetter. Her publicity vehicles were magazines and newspapers, so there were fewer channels, but they were effective. The big differences between Edie's experience and Katia's are due to social media. Katia's Instagram account has some seventy thousand followers, mainly other teenage girls, and it has turned her into a businesswoman. She mixes daily Instagram "stories"—images that disappear after a day—with postings, which are permanent, and more permanent stories that are linked to work—products she is selling or places she has been. In addition she has a YouTube channel where she interacts directly with her fan base.

So what Katia does mixes modeling, lifestyle, style advice, personal information, and opinions. The result is that she is much more in control of how she presents herself and she's not dependent on the agency or any one source. As she gets more followers, more companies send her things to show on Instagram, to model, and to wear. She shows the products faithfully every day and tells her followers where they can buy them. Companies nowadays have people dedicated to following influencers and choosing which ones best suit their brand. The greater the influencer's following, the more brands use her, so Katia tries to make her stories interesting and build her fan base. Sometimes her success with a brand on her Instagram account has led to modeling jobs with the brand, a dynamic that has other commercial ramifications. Thus when the apartment got to be too full of all the clothes she receives, she set up a pop-up store with four or five fellow-influencers and sold everything. Now someone has invented a company to do that—an online outlet store for influencers. You can see what she has for sale.

Katia has also designed some jewelry and sells it directly, and lately she has gone in another direction: she sang a song a couple of months ago at a friend's studio, who video-recorded it. Now she is singing and appearing on music videos, working with Warner Brothers and well-known performers.

The drama at home is to get her to pay more attention to her university work, because she is so tired from all these other activities. However, in a European culture where there is little opportunity for teenagers to earn money, Katia has quite a good income from all this activity.

The essentials don't change, Alice. Beauty is power. But the ways that gets expressed have shifted enormously.

And if you think that's quite a story, listen to this one: there's a nine-year-old boy in Texas by the name of Ryan Kaji who has made nearly thirty million dollars in a year as a "child influencer" reviewing toys and games on YouTube. According to the story I read, he got started at the age of four when, after watching other toy review channels, he asked his mother,

"How come I'm not on YouTube when all the other kids are?" and for three years in a row now he's been the highest-paid YouTuber. That child is the Mozart of influencers.

Clearly, to be a successful influencer you need to perceive possibilities, understand how to exploit them, and work really hard, and none of that was in Edie's nature. She simply didn't think that way. But Andy did, and after he got shot in 1968 he proclaimed that "Business Art is a much better thing to be making than Art Art, because Art Art doesn't support the space it takes up." Duchamp was thinking about art when he bought the urinal, titled it *Fountain*, and submitted it to the Society of Independent Artists' salon, but Andy turned that around, saying anything could be art if you just called it that, including the business he wanted to do anyway.

Now even our *attention* is monetized. I don't think even Andy could have anticipated that, although I've learned that you can never overestimate him.

Andy was naïve at the beginning, so he had a lot to figure out as he went along, but one thing about him, he always lived according to things as they were. That was his great strength: he took what came. As Gretchen Berg put it, "He believed you shouldn't alter the way things really are . . . They have to happen just the way things happen even if it happened to himself."

Another big piece of Andy's attitude was the insight that came to him in the summer of 1956 when he was traveling round the world with Charles Lisanby. He was in love with Charles, and he was suffering torments because nothing was happening between them; in fact, I don't know if anything ever did happen. But then he made this discovery:

> Sometimes people let the same problems make them miserable for years when they could just say, "So what." That's one of my favorite things to say. "So what." . . .
>
> I don't know how I made it through all the years before I learned to do that trick. It took me a long time to learn it, but once you do you never forget.
>
> What makes a person spend time being sad when they could be happy? I was in the Far East and I was walking down a path, and there was a big happy party going on, and actually they were burning a person to death. They were having a party, singing and dancing.

What could be more useful than Andy's trick? It spares you all kinds of suffering, and it's the perfect antidote if, for instance, people are telling you what matters and what you should and shouldn't do. It's also very helpful for someone like me who tends to hyperventilate about things. It's all in how you think about it; just say "So what."

The funny thing is, that's precisely what I thought about when I first saw his work; I thought it showed the kind of flattening of affect that comes when you say "So what."

Andy was constantly making adjustments; he was always finding ways to make himself less vulnerable. Something is tormenting you? Just say "So what." You have difficulty expressing yourself in public? Let Henry Geldzahler say it for you, or Edie. The film you just made turns out to have a big defect? Don't get all upset—use it anyway, take it as it comes. Take everything as it comes.

Think of all the time we waste wishing things were otherwise than they are. Worse yet, *believing* that they're otherwise. Because things really are as they are, and I think one thing that set Andy apart and made him so effective was that he understood that. He actually lived by it.

Because Andy lived in the future and knew it, he sensed not only what the public was seeking but also what it was ready for. He was both the herald and the instigator of a whole lot of change, and that was a big part of his relevance.

Around 1960, when he was so eager to be accepted into the art world, they told him he looked too "swish," that he'd have to put on the three-piece suit and act straight like Robert Rauschenberg and Jasper Johns. Now, Andy really admired those two artists, and he envied them their status. He wanted that acceptance more than anything in life—but not at that price. He went right on acting "swish," and no one who had known him at Carnegie Tech would have been the least bit surprised. In 1947, during the high season of America's homophobia, Andy got a summer job doing displays for an upscale department store in Pittsburgh called Horne's, and you know how he spent his earnings? He bought himself a pink corduroy suit. So he had always flown the flag, and he never stopped flying it. That time when he was being interviewed on WBAI and Henry intervened and explained what he meant, the announcer said at the end, "We've been talking to Mr. Henry Geldzahler and Mr. Andy"—and according to Henry, "Andy grabs the mike and says, 'Please, Miss Andy Warhol.'"

Moreover, it wasn't just his attitude, it was also the ambience of the Factory, where the presence of the gaudy drag queens and gay speed freaks contributed to all manner of Dionysian revels. As Billy Name put it, "[T]he Factory had so many denizens who were the epitome of their lifestyle that it did deal with sex, sexual matters, sexual orientation, sadism and masochism, all the elements that were floating through the culture at the time." On top of that it was the films that Andy made in the early sixties. *Kiss*, for instance, consists of a series of individual three-minute reels of couples kissing: boys kissing girls, girls kissing boys, girls kissing girls, and boys kissing boys. Apparently, when they showed the series in the Factory it was all very dreamlike, because the reels were filmed at twenty-four frames per second and shown at sixteen to evoke the old silent films and the glamour of early Hollywood. (I finally saw it a few years ago, and I have to admit I got pretty bored, but maybe they showed it too fast.) Then there's *Screen Test #2*, in which the fabulous female impersonator Mario Montez imitates his/her idol, the actress Maria Montez, so movingly that he/she really does give off a kind of mysterious glamour. Plus, there's all the famous joke porn, like *Blow Job*, which simply records the face of a young man responding to what you know is going on off-screen, until that's over and he lights a cigarette; and *Mario Banana*, in which Mario Montez, reclining seductively in a white frock and a fuzzy white wig with a big jewel in it, peels a banana and mouths it lasciviously while looking steadily at the viewer from under lowered lids and lashes as thick as twigs. And finally, there's *Couch*, another compendium of individual reels, in which the Factory couch (the one they had before the big one that Billy Name dragged up from the street) is the setting and the subject is sex. Here's what Steven Watson says of it: "As erotica, *Couch* cuts against one's expectations. In the early segments men and women sit on the couch in various states of dress, hardly relating to one another. The reels are filled with tender and homely moments, provided especially by Ondine— kissing Gerard, throwing a scarf over his naked body, wearing his glasses while performing oral sex—that defy standard porno. The film treats sex like an ordinary daily activity, such as eating or smoking."

Exactly: Andy showed that sex of every kind between couples and combinations of every kind was just an ordinary, matter-of-fact, human activity, and to my mind that was a big step in the direction of liberation.

Of course, Andy's attitude also meant that he took people as they came; every human being was remarkable in his eyes. By the same token he tolerated all kinds of behavior. He was unfazed, for instance, when a woman he knew dropped into the Factory one morning with her dog and asked if she could shoot his *Marilyns*. Andy said he didn't mind, and she took out a pistol and shot a whole stack of them right through the head. At first Andy was taken aback that she really did it, then he retitled the pictures *Shot Marilyns* and sold every single one.

But then, of course, Valerie Solanas shot *him*, and after that he was quite different and so was the Factory.

People could have learned a useful lesson from Andy if they had only followed his example, because if you take things as they come, you stay in touch with reality, and that gives you control. However, they already had their eyes on the image. It was the image that counted; it still counts, and reality seems to be beside the point, or rather it operates independently.

Andy wouldn't be surprised. He said, "Nowadays if you're a crook you're still up-there. You can write books, go on TV, give interviews—you're a big celebrity and nobody even looks down on you . . . You're still up-there. This is because more than anything people just want stars." In other words, the star image is what the public wants, and nothing about the real person matters, because fantasy supplies everything.

When Edie moved to New York and began lighting up parties on the Upper East Side, a lot of people saw her as a kind of enchanting Peter Pan figure out of Neverland. That's how Jean Stein saw her, and when Edie died Jean wanted her destroyer brought to justice. That's what she said when she called me one day in the fall of 1972, and what she believed was that Andy Warhol had destroyed Edie. Come to find out, some people still believe that, but they are dead wrong. It should be clear by now that what destroyed Edie were all the forces that made it inevitable that she would destroy herself. Another thing people still believe is that Andy dumped Edie. The opposite is true: she dumped him; not only that, she did it in public at dinner at the Ginger Man one night in late January 1966. Edie was crying and carrying on about how Andy wouldn't let her get close to him, and suddenly she said she didn't want him showing his films of her anymore because they made her look ridiculous. Then she announced that Dylan's people were going to make a film and she was supposed to star in it with him, and now he was coming to meet her, so she had to leave. Dylan came, and she stood up and walked out with him in front of everybody, leaving Andy bright red in the face. He was hurt and humiliated, and although Edie continued to stop by the Factory, it was the end of the close connection between them. But what Jean believed was that Andy had used Edie and thrown her away, and that was the story she was expecting to work on when she called me.

I imagine she started with me because she and I had been friends since boarding school, although we had not seen each other for a while, and as I think about it now, I realize that if anyone else had called me wanting to know about Edie I would have refused to speak to them. Instead, I told Jean to take the train to Hudson and I would meet her there. And for the next eight or nine years she and I talked and talked. Inevitably, since the story is what it is, many of the things I told Jean I have retold here. I gave her all kinds of names and those names led her to others, and the same happened with almost every contact she made. When it came down to it, a lot of people were horrified to see what they had said and refused to let it be published, while others (like Edie's nurse Nan Meikle) asked to be disguised behind pseudonyms. I myself talked so much that in the end (without informing me until it was done) Jean and George Plimpton wound up distributing my testimony among a lot of other voices, but I recognize my own words, and I take responsibility for them. I am ashamed to see the shallow things I said about Andy Warhol. I just didn't get it, and I'm not too sure what Jean got, but she spent many hundreds of hours interviewing anyone she could track down who was in any way connected to Edie Sedgwick or might cast light on the context.

So the coincidence of that old friendship formed the basis of a book that sought to capture the figure of Edie and wound up casting light not only on her and the culture around Andy Warhol but also on a whole lot else that was going on in America at that particular moment. Edie's reach was extraordinary; she managed to wander into a very wide variety of scenes that made up that moment, and Jean investigated every one of them. She began with our family and its history and Edie's early life, and she moved on to cover most of 1960s New York: the uptown milieu and the celebrity world that Jean herself shared with people like Fred and Isabel Eberstadt, which overlapped with the gay celebrity world of Truman Capote and Gore Vidal and the fashion world of Diana Vreeland and Ken Lane; then there was the art world and the Factory and the people in it, from the Cambridge contingent to fixtures like Gerard and Ondine and Billy Name, and later superstars like Viva. Plus, there were all kinds of significant figures of the moment, such as Bob Dylan and Allen Ginsberg and John Cage and even Andy himself, who refused to be interviewed but she managed to get to him anyway because she was just so persistent, and then of course, the whole world of drugs, beginning with the people who passed through the offices of that fancy uptown acid-and-vitamins doctor they call Dr. Roberts, arriving frantic for a shot and floating out afterward with all the time in the world, and then the Chelsea Hotel, where Edie set her room on fire. And throughout it all there was the figure of George Plimpton, whose family were lifelong close friends of our parents, so he knew us all, and he also knew everyone and everything going on in New York. George's reach was almost as wide as Edie's, which is why I suggested his name to Jean when she couldn't fashion a narrative out of all the disparate material she'd accumulated, and it turned out he could and did help make it all into a book. In New York alone, the parade of characters is endless, and then you have the Kennedys and their crowd at Hyannis Port and whoever it was in the Hamptons, and eventually all sorts of different people in California, ranging from a bunch of bikers to the *Ciao! Manhattan* folks and that wonderful actor Michael J. Pollard and even Lance Loud, and last of all Edie's very young husband of a few months, a student named Michael Post, who was there in the bed when she died.

So although Jean started out thinking in terms of Neverland and Peter Pan, every lead she pursued, every voice she listened to with her limitless patience and empathy, contributed to a very different, very complicated and painful story, in which there is not one trace of make-believe. That hasn't stopped people from thinking of Edie in those terms, however.

The irony is that Edie had no interest whatever in make-believe. It was *herself* she wanted to display, *herself* she was desperate to communicate, and the truth is, she simply *was*

213

herself. She was a narcissist through and through, and in New York she would spend long hours every day putting on her makeup and getting ready, and then out she would go and do whatever she felt like, wherever she went. She didn't just want people to see her, she wanted them to listen, and listen up. She wasn't trying to create an image—quite the opposite; she never pretended to be anything but herself. It never crossed her mind to conceal her faults—all her friends said what a liar and a thief she was—and she never wanted to live "as if"; that's precisely what she was trying to escape. All she wanted was to live her own real life and be taken seriously for who she was. I honestly don't think she gave a thought to her social image. Toward the end she even regretted having made a mask of her face with all that makeup.

What Andy wanted for his part was to be famous, but himself was not what he wanted people to see. His sense of existence was so tenuous, he was afraid to fall asleep lest he die, and he said he was always sure that when he looked in the mirror there would be nothing there. Plus, he was hypersensitive and shy to a degree that was crippling, so he developed that artificial manner and made stuff up whenever he was questioned just to protect himself, in effect putting up his hat on a stick. And that allowed him to observe unnoticed, as if from a distance. As Charles Henri Ford put it, Andy "cultivated that cool surface in order to be exposed to more as a spectator."

Andy can be really unreliable when it comes to facts, but at the same time he represents himself intentionally with every word he says or Pat Hackett chooses to include, because that's what he cared about. It matters to me whether he and Edie met in January or in March, and whether she had a cast on her arm or her leg, or not at all, but such things didn't matter to Andy, and he could be pretty cavalier. If you bear that in mind, along with the fact that most of the time he's trying to maintain his personal space and manage the impression he's making, Andy's own writings and interviews are a mine of information. So are all the countless interviews with his close friends and associates, each of whom has his or her own distinct voice and point of view, some more self-interested than others. The best are the ones like Ondine who are not self-interested at all. On top of that you have all the documentation, all the tape recordings and transcripts and the countless photographs that Stephen Shore and Billy Name took, as well as those of the British photographer David McCabe, who documented Andy's life daily for the whole year, 1964–1965. And then there are all the articles and books and exhibition catalogues, as well as several biographies and tons of specialized studies, not to mention everything you can find online. Finally, and on top of it all, you have the Andy Warhol Museum in Pittsburgh, which contains not just works of art but also mountains of evidence of every conceivable kind, including all the boxes of ephemera that Andy called *Space Capsules* and most of the films, even things like a stuffed Great Dane from his collection and the letter that Edie wrote to him after he got shot.

The biographies and many of the interviews cast light on the complexities of Andy's behavior, but that's not what I am interested in here. Instead, I am trying to learn about his deeper nature, and these are the major voices I listen to:

Gerard Malanga, who was present at everything and gave

215

careful and straightforward answers to every question an interviewer ever asked him, although he had to stop a few years ago because it was taking over his life.

Billy Name, who is so sound and direct always in what he says about Andy, about himself, and about the Factory.

Charles Henri Ford, who knew Andy early on.

Henry Geldzahler, although he's complicated, because he was Andy's closest friend and companion and the principal influence on his work from the day they met in July 1960 until five or six years later, when Henry was about to move a new lover in, meaning he wouldn't be available anymore to talk on the phone first thing every morning and again last thing at night.

There's also Gretchen Berg, that very young journalist to whom Andy opened up so unexpectedly; she describes him as a very simple man and says he was "capable of . . . great sensitivity and thoughtfulness . . . and a certain insight . . . into other people"; plus she calls him "a very serious guy . . . and very shrewd . . . completely detached from the things that were going on around him."

Then there's Ondine, whose take on Andy is at once deep and simple; he meant it when he said, "He's a very feeling, a very caring, a very *human* person."

And Stephen Shore, who told me that he learned how to be an artist from watching Andy, seeing how he made choices.

And finally Lou Reed of the Velvet Underground, although he didn't enter the Factory or start collaborating with Andy until December 1965, when Edie was already drifting downward and away. He too had a wonderful, deep take on Andy, and it's clear he had nothing but the greatest respect for him.

He said what he learned from Andy was how to be a nice person, and that work is the whole story; he tells you all about him in *Songs for Drella*.

Above all, there's Andy's own voice, which I trust even when it's rendered by Pat Hackett to present him as he wished to sound, because he knows what he wants to communicate. With Andy it's not the words that count.

To most people Andy presented himself as a vague, recessive figure: he was always asking for ideas and wondering what somebody else thought, always noncommittal when asked his own opinion. Who would ever have guessed that he was actually well read and widely informed? Or that he went regularly to church? Or what an extraordinarily hard worker he was, and that behind the façade he was altogether present and so intensely purposeful?

It's strange, but for the limited period of their association I feel I know Andy better than I ever knew Edie. I know *about* her, but I don't know her. Not even Jean Stein's oral history captures her, despite the great multitude of different voices she enlisted, including my own, all of us trying so hard to tell the truth about Edie and what happened. All you get is kaleidoscopic glimpses, sightings, as it were, and you can never get close. Two things I know now that I didn't before are what a powerful presence she had and how effectively she could handle herself (while she still could, I mean). And yet I sense that there was something ambiguous about her presence, as if it was powerful and at the same time quite empty. Andy himself said she was a wonderful, beautiful blank; she could be whatever you wanted her to be. To put it metaphorically, Edie was like a particle of light, all energy and no mass. The one fixed thing about her was her image, and I think it's a big key to her importance, because before you knew it people were wanting not only to look at images like hers, they wanted to be images themselves.

It's true that self-invention and reinvention had always been part of the American repertory, but that is for individuals wanting a fresh start—a new life, a new career, a whole new persona—in the land of promise. This image business is altogether different, because as far as I can see the commodified self is a pure product of the consumer culture and the huge wave of narcissism it has generated.

Sometime in the seventies, the *New York Times* added sections to the paper titled "Weekend" and "Living" and "Home," and Nora Ephron went over there to see what was going on. An executive in the business department told her exactly: he said the biggest psychographics right now were self-improvement and self. ("Psychographics"? That right there tells you what's going on.) "Self is very strong," were the man's actual words. So: the *Times* was rushing to address this brand-new market, the self that wanted to create an image for the public to see.

Now full-page ads began appearing that showed groups of tanned and windblown models on docks or grassy dunes, girls with blue eyes and straight brown hair in dead-simple clothes, and good-looking boys to match. The point was that you too could look as if you came from one of those old-money enclaves on the Eastern Seaboard; it was just a matter of purchasing the look. The designer was called Ralph Lauren, and it wasn't long before he was offering home furnishings and all manner of scenography to support looking "as if." He understood that people were seeking to remake themselves into images—he had done it himself—and what he understood made him a billionaire and a big celebrity.

In the seventies, while Nora Ephron was drawing attention to signs of this new preoccupation with the self in everything from journalism to the women's movement, I was working for a publication that covered the current bibliography in the field of art history, and even there we were seeing the same thing. Certain art historians were acting like celebrities, a particular museum director became a huge celebrity for introducing consumerism into his august institution, and traditional academic authors were suddenly writing in the first person about how Renaissance artists managed their images. Self-fashioning was a big topic.

At the same time we began to see a lot about appropriation in art, which if you think about it also involves the introduction—or rather the superimposition—of the self. It was nothing new; Duchamp raised the issue with his *Ready-mades* and Rauschenberg had been incorporating found objects into his work for a while, but now postmodern architects were using citations all over the place, and artists were making something called "appropriation art." Again, Duchamp had started it by appropriating the *Mona Lisa*, and in 1963 Andy Warhol rang changes on Duchamp's idea by making a whole bunch of *Mona Lisas*, setting them up in a grid, and calling the picture

*30 Are Better Than One.* Around that same time, he told Gene Swenson one reason he used silk screens was that he thought somebody should be able to do all his paintings for him; he thought it would be great if more people took up silk screens so no one would know whether a picture was his or someone else's. It's not surprising, then, that in the late spring of 1965, when he was back from showing his *Flowers* in Paris, he gave one of his silk screens to an appropriation artist called Elaine Sturtevant so she could produce her own versions. Which she promptly did and showed them right away at the Bianchini Gallery in New York. Now, Andy's *Flower* paintings were based on a photograph that Henry Geldzahler picked out of a magazine, and what that means is that in giving Sturtevant his silk screen Andy created an image indirectly by enabling her to make an image of an image that he had made from yet another image by yet another artist, a photographer called Patricia Caulfield, who sued him when she found out. The critics said Sturtevant was exploring the issues of authenticity, celebrity, and the creative process, when in a sense it was really Andy Warhol who appropriated Sturtevant. On top of it he was amusing himself by referring interviewers to her when they asked about his technique.

Not surprisingly, art criticism was also showing the impact of the new preoccupation with the self. The first indication I remember spotting was a column in *Arts Magazine* that consisted of nothing but extracts from the diary of a young art historian and critic called Robert Pincus-Witten. It was all about his day, what he did and where he went, who he saw, the parties and openings he attended, the artists' studios he visited. In other words, not a word of art criticism, nothing but pure first-person singular, pure gossip, and a lot of what I considered to be showing off.

Pincus-Witten was also the author of an article about a rising young sculptor called Lynda Benglis that appeared in *Artforum* in 1974 together with a centerfold advertisement paid for by the artist herself. It was meant as a statement, but that ad remains a perfect lesson in how to become a notorious celebrity: it shows Benglis standing there stark naked except for her white-framed sunglasses, through which she's issuing a brassy look over her shoulder. She stands sideways, with one hand on her hip and the other holding an extra-long, super-realistic dildo that sticks straight out of her dark brown pubic hair. The ad was Benglis's response to a poster by Robert Morris called *Labyrinths*, in which he appears sideways, naked to the waist, wearing a black metal helmet, a studded steel collar, steel cuffs, and great loops of chain draped over his muscular arms and chest; he too looks straight at you through dark glasses, only his are aviator and hers are harlequin.

And now a whole generation of other artist-celebrities emerged, ranging from Jeff Koons, another notorious celebrity, to the tragic young graffiti artist Jean-Michel Basquiat, who Andy teamed up with for a time in the eighties. The two of them produced quite a body of work together.

The silk-screen paintings that Andy produced in the sixties—everything from the *Elvises* and *Marilyns* and *Mona Lisas* to the *Most Wanted Men* and the *Death and Disaster* pictures—were all based on existing images. But at the time that wasn't what I noticed; I was still thinking in terms of the past, so for instance I made a mistake when I saw *Mustard Race Riot*, which consists of two panels, one with the image and one blank. I thought the point was to remind the viewer that the picture was an image created by an artist, like Magritte's *Ceci n'est pas une pipe*. Come to find out, Andy added the extra panel so he could put the price up. Similarly, I remember being unsettled by *Lavender Disaster* because it represented the electric chair at Sing Sing before the Rosenbergs were executed. I assumed it was a political statement, but it seems I was mistaken. Apparently, the reason Andy painted all those *Deaths and Disasters* was that Henry Geldzahler showed him the newspaper headline *129 Die in Jet* and said that was enough of soups and Coke bottles, "it was time for some death."

. . . However, with Andy you never know, it needn't have been either/or, it could very easily have been both, because his tactics of distancing and estrangement enabled him to take a subject and repropose it on totally new terms. There was the real Andy and there was the cool Andy, his hat on the stick.


Putting up your hat on a stick is the opposite of living "as if"; it's a way of protecting real life, whereas living and looking "as if" means living to one degree or another in unreality. It's all about creating and presenting an image, and it turns the rest of the world into a mirror for the self. The assumption is, "If I appear to be a certain kind of person, people will see me as that kind of person, and it will be as if I were that kind of person." Most people living "as if" aren't trying actively to suppress reality, they just want to cover it with something they think looks sexier.

In the case of our family, however, suppressing reality was the whole point. It was the premise upon which our parents constructed their life, and ours with it: the object was to establish and sustain our father in a manner that would protect and fulfill him. As a young man he had started out with enormous ambition and a lot of promise, determined to make his mark on the world, but his mental fragility prevented him from fulfilling any of it. He fell back on being an artist, which as far as the world and life in Long Island were concerned meant he shunted himself off the main track and onto a spur, so he was much happier being a rancher in what was then a remote valley in California. That was the life that suited him best anyway. Still, he never ceased to be proud and ambitious, and he and our mother wound up putting all they had, humanly and materially, into protecting him and building him up into the image of a Renaissance man: an artist, writer, patron of institutions and the arts, who was also a rancher, a spectacular physical specimen and potent father of eight, living an ideal life in an ideal setting; and in that they succeeded. They did so with the support of money and class, and by ignoring reality and the human needs of their children. Inevitably, as time went by, reality and the distress of some of the children began to manifest themselves, but for many crucial years nothing showed through; even after the Groton letter, which should have demonstrated once and for all that my father was not what he appeared to be, the image persisted.

And meanwhile, unbeknownst to our parents, society was changing; the closed world of inherited class in which they were raised and for which they believed they were raising us was no longer intact. So while they continued to live "as if," one by one we children left the ranch for a world in which what we had been taught to expect, everything that was meant to be fixed and unquestionable, was breaking up and disappearing in the current of time. We were not the only ones who had trouble finding a footing, but what happened to our family is cautionary: it proves that things really are the way they are and they unfold accordingly.

I'm sure one reason why Edie flourished in Andy's orbit was that he never lived "as if," and that's not the only way the Factory was the mirror opposite of the ranch. Both were worlds unto themselves, each with a central figure, but one was constructed as a static ideal world, and the other was a constantly fluctuating nexus of personalities and circumstance. The ranch was a vast and sparsely inhabited space, closed and exclusive, while the Factory was one densely populated floor of a medium-sized building in a very large city, and it was wide open and inclusive to a fault, given that Andy wound up getting shot. Each of the two worlds was dominated by a powerful male figure, one gregarious and priapic, the other shy and deliberately "swish." Both men were artists, one representing the fading academic past, the other the dynamic present; one with no influence whatsoever, the other on the point of becoming the most influential artist of the time. And finally, drugs were a factor in both worlds, only on the ranch they were respectably obtained by prescription, while in the Factory, they were mostly provided by Rotten Rita.

Edie went from one world to the other without ever really leaving the ranch. She just took the ratio to her surroundings that she had established at home and extended it to whatever new context she found herself in—Cambridge, New York, the Factory, the whole wide world. She had been dominant from childhood, so it was only natural that she should be dominant wherever she was, and for that brief period in 1965 she was dominant and very conspicuous, in the Factory and fashionable arenas of New York City, and in the media as well. With Edie, dominance was not a matter of ambition—that only entered her mind when others put it there—it was simply a gift that she had always had. She was born with it.

Dominance came naturally to Andy as well, but at the same time he was deliberately self-effacing. As he put it: "I've always had a conflict because I'm shy and yet I like to take up a lot of personal space." That's why he had to put up his hat on a stick: to give himself room to manage his shyness in public and to observe in privacy. Moreover, he didn't just want to observe, he wanted to capture everything he observed that he found interesting. Thus, for instance, when Freddie Herko danced out the window to the sound of Mozart's *Coronation Mass* and landed five stories down on Cornelia Street, Andy said he wished he'd been there to film it.

So it's not really surprising that when he got that video camera on loan from *Tape Recording Magazine*, his first response was, Now you could film your own death.

Think about it: right away he envisaged not only the "selfie" but also the ultimate reality show.

The first time I saw someone take a selfie I had no idea what I was seeing. We were in Portugal and had taken a picnic to the beach to watch the sun set. Then, just as it was slipping into the sea and setting the waves on fire, a man came running down onto the sand, turned around, held up his cell phone for a second or two, and ran back up to the restaurant. He never stopped to look, so I figured he was just in a hurry. But then a few days later we were in Lisbon with friends, looking at a little Rubens oil sketch in the Gulbenkian Museum, and a woman got right in front of us. She held up her phone and photographed first the label and then the picture; then she turned around, photographed herself with the picture, and moved on to the next one. She too didn't look. She didn't experience her own experience; all she did was record it. I was told she was taking something called "selfies" (I can't help it; to me that word always carries a whiff of the masturbatory) to post on the internet for her "followers" to see.

So there was a new kind of self-portrait that you could make with your portable phone and display to the world on the internet. I confess I didn't see much point to it. I actually thought it might be a fad, but of course it proliferated, and now people all over the world are busy creating images that add up to stories about themselves. Some just want to share their lives, but there are many who really enjoy making believe and showing off. Everywhere I go I see people with their phones out, because if they're not looking and posting and texting, they are either talking or just checking, and meanwhile, the time they have to live is passing. I know what it's like, because I myself have a cell phone now, and although I don't do any following or posting, I can't help taking it out and checking it.

There was no such thing as social media when Andy said that about the video camera, but he sensed what the public was going to want, and it was just a matter of time before the technology caught up. For the reality show, however, the technology already existed, and in 1971 PBS made the very first one. It was a series called *An American Family*, and it was intended to chronicle the daily life of a typical upper-middle-class American family, Pat and Bill Loud of Santa Barbara, California, and their five kids. It was filmed between May and December 1971, and as it turned out, it chronicled the separation and divorce of the parents, as well as the emergence of their twenty-year-old son Lance from the closet. So it really did represent a typical upper-middle-class white family in America, and of all things, Edie was present at one of the last episodes.

Lance Loud coming out on national television in 1971, just two years after Stonewall, made him an instant icon. He was one of those young people who lived in what had recently been the future, and he knew all about Andy and Edie. He was fifteen when his father showed him a picture of the two of them in *Time* magazine and said, "Look at this crazy, crazy, crazy guy." Lance asked what was wrong with him, and his father said, "Well, this guy has dyed his hair silver and his girlfriend has dyed *her* hair silver, and she wears these big ball earrings," and read him the article. That was all it took: Lance fell in love. He said, "They were so non-vocal, and yet it seemed, from what I could tell, they were getting their way . . . really just riding, riding, riding the wild surf of New York society . . . So they became the only hobby I ever had. I went to the library, I read up on Pop Art. I read *everything* I could about Andy Warhol, about his underground Factory . . . As for Edie . . . I thought she was just like the fairy princess of the whole thing." And then Lance began writing letters to Andy, asking what he thought about, who he was going around with, that kind of thing, and eventually he heard back. "It was a crinkled piece of paper inside a big envelope, just a little wadded piece of paper on which was typed: 'My number is . . .' and then his phone number. That was all. My eyes . . . oh, God! . . . my heart, my soul, my toenails started blooming." It took Lance time to work up his courage, he was so overwhelmed, but then they spoke, and for the next few years, every Friday and Saturday in the early hours of the morning Santa Barbara time, Lance would go out, find a pay phone, and call Andy collect, and Andy would be awake to tell him everything he had done. After a time Andy began asking Lance to tell him he loved him, and Lance would say, "I love you, Andy," and Andy would say, "Oh, say it like you *mean* it. Oh, tell me again." But then Andy got shot and changed his number, so for a while that was that. But when Lance went to New York in 1973 he was a celebrity himself, and pretty soon they met at a party and became friends. Lance even wound up writing for *Interview*.

In November 1971, Lance was being filmed for an episode

of *An American Family*, and he wanted to attend a fashion show at the Santa Barbara Museum. He didn't have an invitation, but Edie came to the door; she had spotted him and she had spotted the camera. Lance had seen her, or what was left of her by then, a while before that on the beach at Isla Vista. Imagine the scene: a big German shepherd came lolloping down onto the sand, and after him came Edie in a little brown dress, with flowers in her long dark hair and a bouquet of lilies and weeds in one hand. Everyone on the beach stopped to look as she ran with her dog into the sea. Lance actually spoke to her and she responded, they even kissed, but she said some rude things about fags and he didn't follow up, and now here she was again, coming up to him at the fashion show. Lance said, "She seemed to be grasping that ray from the camera. She just stole the scene." And you know who was there to see it? Tom Goodwin, Edie's friend from her days in Cambridge and the Factory, the guy who crashed her Mercedes. He had a job with the program, and he was there for the filming. Edie didn't remember him right away. It was the camera she connected with, and all evening long she kept coming back to it.

When the show was over, Edie danced with Lance down a long corridor singing, "Looka there, looka there, Young Blood . . . I can't get you outta my mind," then she examined all the beautiful clothes, tried on a red chiffon dress, and praised everything and everybody. Finally, she went off with a bunch of people who were on their way to a party. It was November 15, 1971, the last night of her life. By morning she was dead of an overdose of barbiturates.

On her very last night in this world, Edie wandered into

the original reality show and grasped the ray from the camera. She managed to cast a final flicker of light on herself.

*An American Family* drew ten million viewers, and since then reality shows have proliferated, the audiences for them have grown, and the so-called reality has become more and more problematic. After all, it was a show called *The Apprentice* that took a tabloid celebrity tycoon named Donald Trump, a man who all his life had lived "as if," and transformed him into the image of an extraordinarily powerful and successful businessman. As his biographer Michael D'Antonio put it, Trump "made more money playing a fictional version of himself than he made *being* himself. Make-believe was where he made bank."

This "make-believe" is a whole new dimension, a kind of alternate expanding universe that now emanates from the internet, and I wonder if Andy would have anticipated it; however, he was certainly right about people filming their own deaths. Last August, a thirty-three-year-old veteran named Ronnie McNutt put up a very graphic two-hour live-stream video of his suicide on Facebook. His horrified friends saw it and reported it numerous times while he was still alive, only to be told after his death that the video didn't violate any of what Facebook calls its "community guidelines" . . .

I also wonder what Andy would have done with social media. I can't see him posting images of himself on the internet. He always wanted to be the observer, never the observed, and he was private to the point of being really secretive about his life. So it may surprise you to know that he worked on his body. In fact, by the time he met Edie he had been exercising seriously for several years and taking those prescription diet pills called Obetrol, and he was up to a hundred pull-ups a day. He was happy to *look* "swish"—that was important to him—but he wanted to *be* strong. Andy's interest in his body was one more trait that he and Edie had in common, and the two of them talked a lot on the phone about the exercises they did.

I'm not sure how Edie would handle social media either. I'm thinking of how she appeared in some of Andy's films and McCabe's photographs, wandering about in her tiny black lace bra and panties. She's totally at ease being seen like that, but I doubt if she would have posted images of herself on the internet. On the other hand, she probably wouldn't have minded if others saw her in her underwear and posted the images of what they saw. She never thought about her social image; she let it take care of itself (although she did worry about how she came across in Andy's films because she was so anxious to be taken seriously). Instead, her real preoccupation was her body image. She was so preoccupied with it that whatever she consumed throughout the day—and believe me, she consumed a lot—she would throw up almost all of it in order to keep from getting fat. That's a serious medical condition, and the term for it is "bulimia."

Eating disorders existed in Edie's time, obviously, but they were rare, and little was known about them. It wasn't until the sixties that the first real authority on the subject, a

German-born psychoanalyst called Hilde Bruch, even began to study it. What Dr. Bruch found was that bulimia develops when the mother's responses to signals of need from the child, whether of food or self-expression in general, are either inappropriate or inadequate.

That might apply to Edie, but I wonder whether the main cause of it is still believed to lie in the mother-child relationship. What about society's responses to the needs of a child? Isn't it possible that society's preoccupation with the self and its image might also be contributing to the present plague of eating disorders?

If you think about it, bulimia is pure consumption and waste; the principal symptom is gorging followed by self-induced vomiting, and another symptom is binge-shopping. What a metaphor for our consumer society . . .

Andy shopped on a massive scale. Already in the fifties he was buying works of art and Oriental exotica and antique furniture and objects of high modern design and all manner of oddities such as penny arcade machines and carousel figures and campy items such as a stuffed peacock and the huge mirror ball that became a big feature of the Silver Factory, and all of it wound up in his house. Edie, on the other hand, bought only what she could put on her person, but there never was a more compulsive shopper and spender than she was, and no one who was more cavalier with money. Just to give you one small example, Sterling Morrison described riding in a limousine with Edie one time when she had just bought some expensive shoes at Capezio. "After taking a second look at them," he said, "she decided she didn't like them, rolled down the window, and threw them out." She shopped and she shopped, and when money was short she shoplifted; her closets and drawers were always stuffed to overflowing with brand-new clothes, and there were always boxes everywhere under the furniture. And like Andy himself, she was a real hoarder: she hoarded drugs, she hoarded makeup, she even hoarded brassieres; he said she had around fifty of them in her trunk, in all different colors, all with the price tags still on, all A-cup. Incidentally, Edie hated having those tiny breasts, and after she moved back to California, she got silicone implants to make them big and round. She was the first person I ever heard of who did that, and now women are augmenting everything from their lips to their bottoms.

I don't know just when Edie would have been well enough to have the surgery, because after she walked out on Andy in January 1966 her downward spiral accelerated, and she was in and out of hospitals for what remained of her life. She did have a few pretty good months in Dylan's orbit that spring—this was the period in which Dylan recorded "Just Like a Woman" and his associate Bob Neuwirth made a film with Edie and they began a tumultuous affair—but then in the fall of '66 she fell asleep with a lighted cigarette and set her apartment on fire; the whole building had to be evacuated. After that she moved to the Chelsea Hotel, and six months later she did it again and, miraculously, escaped with nothing worse than badly burned hands. And yet, and yet, she still had enough magic that Bob Margouleff and David Weisman managed to film the first part of *Ciao! Manhattan* with her that same spring, the part in black and white; and in August, despite the drugged and bedraggled state in which she arrived, Richard Leacock starred her in the film sequences he made for Sarah Caldwell's production of *Lulu* by Alban Berg at the Boston Opera. Not only that, in the course of making *Ciao! Manhattan*, Edie so enraptured David Weisman that he went on to spend years working with her to complete the film (alas, the results, in lurid color, were pitiful). This took place in California, because in the fall of 1968, a year after Fuzzy died, my mother flew east and took Edie out of Manhattan State, where she had been committed, and home to the ranch. Edie seemed to do a bit better and even had her own place in Isla Vista for a while, but she kept fetching up in the hospital in Santa Barbara—in fact, it's where she met her future husband, who was also in treatment for addiction—and between times she worked with David Weisman, who never stopped believing in her. After Edie died, he spent I don't know how long on a project for a documentary film about her, and in 2006 he published a book called *Edie: Girl on Fire*. So despite everything horrific that was going on in her life, Edie still had enough magic to inspire David Weisman, enough magic that everyone on the beach in Isla Vista stopped and looked when she ran into the sea with her dog, enough that she could still capture the camera at the fashion show the night before she died.

Edie and her image continue to be relevant; she is present in the public mind. Everyone seems to know her name:

designers give it to products, every so often there's a magazine article about her and Andy, Jean's book about her is taught in schools, and she even crops up several times a year as a clue in the *New York Times* crossword puzzle. Not too long ago there was a film that attempted to portray her as she was in the Factory. I saw it on a plane, and it was so fake it was painful, not because the actress wasn't serious or talented but because it couldn't be done: only Edie could be as she was.

And listen to this: a couple of months ago I got a letter from a guy somewhere in Missouri—God knows what the connection was or how he found me—on behalf of a young Polish artist who is obsessed with Edie. She had traveled all the way to California to get close to her, she had visited the ranch and the graveyard, she had even gone to the hospital where Edie was born, and along the way she had bought a book, some horse story for children, in a secondhand bookshop in Santa Barbara. The dedication on the flyleaf read "Given to Edie Sedgwick by her sister Alice." It was written in pencil in a childish hand that was not Edie's and certainly not mine, and what they wanted was for me to authenticate it. Of course, I couldn't; anyone who was not blinded by wishful thinking would have recognized that inscription as an opportunistic forgery. But what about the story?

All along I had been operating on the assumption that if people had only known Edie as she really was, and especially if they had known what a horrific life she actually led, they would not have responded to her as they did. And even when Jean's book came out and everybody knew all about it, and they responded to her more than ever, it never once crossed my mind that it could be precisely *because* of that horrific life.

We have a new neighbor up the road by the lake, and when my son ran into her recently on a hike, he happened to mention what I was up to. Her response was so astonishing that he called to tell me about it. He said she had to stop and take it in, she was so stunned by the coincidence, because she had known about Edie her whole entire life and had identified with her from childhood, long before she read Jean's book. Then when she did read it at the age of fourteen, she became so obsessed that the following year she painted a large black-and-white image of Edie's head, the one from the *Ciao! Manhattan* poster, on the wall of her bedroom.

My neighbor's name is Kate. I went to see her, and here's what she told me:

Kate was the youngest of four children of a family doctor and his wife, a sculptor, and they lived in Philadelphia. Kate's mother, who was roughly Edie's age, had been a prodigy and grew up idolizing Kerouac and the Beat poets, entranced with the whole idea of the counterculture and expanding your consciousness with drugs, and she knew all about Andy Warhol, the Factory, and Edie Sedgwick. As for her father, according to Kate he was a functioning alcoholic and in her words, an "exercise bulimic." The couple started out in Philadelphia and after the children were born their father decided to move them all to a rural area in southern New Jersey, where he took up a practice and they lived a rather romantic upper-class life—Kate actually called it living "as if"—in a large house with an attached structure that became her mother's studio. Her mother spent her days in that studio producing art, and as the children grew she attended less and less to her maternal and domestic responsibilities, although they would give grand parties for as many as a hundred people. The family spent their summers at the shore in Ocean City, in a colony of close friends, all with children, where a great deal of drinking went on.

However, the couple had trouble staying together, and when Kate was thirteen they finally divorced. The older children were away in college, so Kate fetched up alone with her mother in a three-storey converted glove factory in a changing neighborhood in Philadelphia. She was sent to public school, where she immediately went from drinking to hard drugs. At the same time her mother began acting more like a peer and treated Kate as a fellow adventurer rather than a teenager in need of parenting. Kate responded by becoming seriously addicted to alcohol and drugs, and deeply anorexic. This was when she read Jean's book. The next year, when she was fifteen, her mother took off for Europe with her married boss, leaving Kate at home with her close friend Elizabeth, who was the daughter of a family from the Ocean City community. Elizabeth was eighteen and a freshman in college, and as it happened she too was into drugs. So first thing you know both girls dropped out of school, and from then on they did nothing but drugs.

Furthermore, Elizabeth was also obsessed with Edie, and she helped Kate paint the mural of Edie's face on the bedroom wall. Months went by, and one day Kate's mother walked in without warning and wept at what she saw, because the place was completely trashed.

Kate managed to complete school early, and at age sixteen she moved alone to London to pursue a career in acting and dance; instead she wound up addicted and homeless. Someone brought her back to Philadelphia, and when she was eighteen a judge sent her to a long-term high-security ward in a mental hospital, which she said was more like a prison. A year later, with the help of Elizabeth, who was now in recovery herself, and a very special visiting medical student from South Africa who was doing a rotation at the hospital, Kate entered a twelve-step program and began her recovery.

I asked Kate what it was about Edie, and she gave me a number of answers:

- She wanted to *be* Edie, to be someone whose suffering people cared about.
- Part of Edie's draw was that she had everything and couldn't value or access it.
- She identified with Edie because she too had been raised living "as if."

- Edie was a *she*, and all the writers Kate read and met were men, Beat men.
- Kate too was anorexic and addicted.
- She was starved for attention and saw that Edie knew how to get it.
- Edie gave her permission to live nihilistically, narcissistically, without caring about anyone or anything.
- Kate imagined she would be like Edie, that she would be glamorous and famous and die a glamorous death.
- Finally, Kate said she wanted to be on the front page when she killed herself; that's what she was planning. It was the only thing that mattered to her, and the judge took it all away when he sentenced her to that mental institution. (He took it away for good: Kate was sober, in AA, and in college by the age of nineteen.)

How could I not have known that of *course* Edie would be a powerful model for any narcissistic, self-destructive girl, particularly one addicted to drugs, particularly one with an eating disorder, particularly one with talent and ambition? How could I not have understood that?

It's clear, then, along with her image, Edie herself has always been wholly relevant. It remains unclear, at least to me, what it was that made her extraordinary. The mystifying thing is that no one can tell me, not even Stephen Shore, who saw her every single day for months and months in the Factory and recorded her presence in countless photographs—not even he could tell me. He said it was all very long ago and he couldn't remember, but he thought it was significant that she appears in more of his photographs than anyone else . . . And Randy Bourscheidt, a friend of Andy's who saw Edie several times a week for close to a year, in the Factory, at Max's Kansas City, and all around town, couldn't tell me either. All he could say was that she was beautiful, she had a special relationship to Andy, she was not social, he didn't remember her speaking, he got the sense that she was solitary. And then he said, "She could be known only by what she evoked in others."

And in fact the only direct evidence I have of the effect Edie had is that one moment in *a: a novel* when she comes into the Factory after the video camera has been delivered and Andy and Ondine are so excited to see her.

Listen to them, how excited they are:

[ONDINE:] Oh, Bonjourno! Oh.
[DRELLA:] Oh the movie's here, the camera. No, how
    was your, our day? Hey, . . . I'm following Ondine
    today, Taxi. (*Ondine sings.*) Taxi I'm following On-
    dine today.

. . . And then her conversation is so boring, so self-centered, so very banal.

The other day, still searching, I took another look at that film about Edie and Andy called *Factory Girl*. What I saw was a perfect demonstration of the fact that a fictional image can never be anything more than that, a fiction, and in this case it was a travesty. Then I watched the video that was made to

coincide with the film, and there were all those familiar figures forty years later—Gerard Malanga, with his curls turned
gray, cut short, and combed; Sam Green, no longer boyish
either, his hair and beard now pure white and immaculately
trimmed; and Danny Fields, whose angular face had quite
filled out. The big surprise was Edie's friend Richie Berlin,
looking like a middle-aged Yankee lady, simply dressed, with
short, straight hair that's still brown, her face minutely wrin-
kled as if from too much time in the sun, and a very clear look
in her sky-blue eyes as she talked. What was striking about the
way every one of them spoke of Edie was how real and immediate she still was in all their minds.

Image of Edie from the *Ciao! Manhattan* poster,
painted by Kate Kohler Amory on her bedroom wall

———

It seems that all the evidence I will ever have of Edie, of the figure that she was and remains, consists of her image and the response that she evoked in others. Is it possible that she was not a superstar, not a real star after all, but more like a celestial body of another kind, composed of dark matter, knowable only by the gravitational pull that she exerted?

I keep thinking about her, and I cannot say.

# NOTES

## THE PAST

38  *She made Edie sit on the potty*: Jean Stein and George Plimpton, *Edie: An American Biography* (New York: Knopf, 1982), 65.

38  *Nan said*: Stein and Plimpton, *Edie*, 65.

80  *As Suky described it*: Stein and Plimpton, *Edie*, 80.

82  *For instance, she told Isabel Eberstadt*: Stein and Plimpton, *Edie*, 228.

106  *This was the beginning*: Melissa Painter and David Weisman, *Edie: Girl on Fire* (San Francisco: Chronicle Books, 2006), 136.

106  *He said she gave him*: Painter and Weisman, *Edie: Girl on Fire*, 81.

109  *One weekend a beau of hers*: Stein and Plimpton, *Edie*, 159–62.

111  *Pretty soon Grandma's lawyer*: Unpublished interview with Melissa Painter.

112  *"The people coming in from Cambridge"*: Andy Warhol and Pat Hackett, *POPism: The Warhol Sixties* (New York: Harper & Row, 1980), 122–23.

112  *Another thing Danny said was*: Warhol and Hackett, *POPism*, 122–23.

114  *But all this time in private*: Stein and Plimpton, *Edie*, 168.

115  *I know they were in close touch*: In the PBS *American Masters* Andy Warhol documentary Paul Morrissey says, "[Edie] had come

back from Woodstock a drug addict, and there wasn't much you could do with her."

## 1965

124   *As Andy put it*: Warhol and Hackett, *POPism*, 139.

124   *"In '65 the tempo"*: PBS *American Masters* Andy Warhol documentary.

124   *She hadn't even known*: Steven Watson, *Factory Made: Warhol and the Sixties* (New York: Pantheon, 2003), 196.

124   *She told the TV host*: *The Merv Griffin Show*, October 6, 1965.

126   *Ondine said that when they saw*: Stein and Plimpton, *Edie*, 232.

127   *As Ronnie Tavel put it*: Patrick S. Smith, *Andy Warhol's Art and Films* (Ann Arbor: U.M.I., 1986), 501.

127   *Because Ronnie Tavel*: Smith, *Warhol's Art and Films*, 95–96.

127   *According to Tavel*: Victor Bockris, *Warhol: The Biography* (New York: Da Capo Press, 2003), 219.

127   *And as Tavel complained*: Smith, *Warhol's Art and Films*, 501.

128   *He says Andy was going around*: Smith, *Warhol's Art and Films*, 501.

128   *It's called* Poor Little Rich Girl: Jonas Mekas, in John Coplans, *Andy Warhol* (Greenwich, CT: New York Graphic Society, 1970), 150–51. Mekas dates *Poor Little Rich Girl* March–April 1965.

131   *Andy said if Edie had needed a script*: Warhol and Hackett, *POPism*, 139.

131   *When Jonas Mekas*: Jonas Mekas, *Movie Journal: The Rise of the New American Cinema, 1959-1971*, 2nd ed. (New York: Columbia University Press, 2016), 193.

131   *Many years later he wrote*: Andy Warhol, *The Philosophy of Andy Warhol (from A to B and Back Again)* (New York: Harcourt, 1975), 27.

133   *He told Old Owl: I'll Be Your Mirror: The Selected Andy Warhol Interviews, 1962-1987*, ed. K. Goldsmith (New York: Carroll & Graf, 2004), 113–14.

133 *One night Jacques Kaplan*: David McCabe and David Dalton, *A Year in the Life of Andy Warhol* (London: Phaidon, 2003), 118–19, 122, 123.

134 *Edie was there*: Warhol and Hackett, *POPism*, 128, 132.

135 *She had already begun wearing*: Warhol and Hackett, *POPism*, 141–42.

135 *You might want to take what he says*: McCabe and Dalton, *Year in the Life*, 180.

135 *Peter Schjeldahl wrote*: Peter Schjeldahl, in "Andy Warhol 1928–87: A Collage of Appreciations from the Artist's Colleagues, Critics and Friends," *Art in America* 75, no. 5 (May 1987): 137.

136 *Steven Watson describes them at the Crazy Horse Saloon*: Watson, *Factory Made*, 207.

136 *He said later*: Warhol and Hackett, *POPism*, 142.

137 *McCabe said he hadn't even known*: Obituary of David McCabe, *New York Times*, March 23, 2021; quote from 2011 interview with the website The Arts Desk.

137 *When the year was up*: Obituary of David McCabe.

138 *David Bourdon saw Andy*: John Wilcock, *The Autobiography and Sex Life of Andy Warhol* (New York: Trela, 2010), 43.

139 *To give you an idea what he was up against*: Bockris, *Warhol: The Biography*, 140.

140 *The poet Charles Henri Ford*: Wilcock, *Autobiography and Sex Life*, 60–61.

140 *Here's what he said about her*: Warhol and Hackett, *POPism*, 137.

141 *Plus, she was cozy*: Painter and Weisman, *Edie: Girl on Fire*, 71.

143 *"Joy" is the word*: Painter and Weisman, *Edie: Girl on Fire*, 85.

143 *It's also the word*: Painter and Weisman, *Edie: Girl on Fire*, 83.

143 *There he talks about*: Stephen Shore and Lynne Tillman, *The Velvet Years: Warhol's Factory, 1965–67* (New York: Thunder's Mouth, 1995), 75–77.

145 *In the words of Andy's friend*: Bockris, *Warhol: The Biography*, 193.

145 *"David Whitney"*: Warhol and Hackett, *POPism*, 126.

148 *According to Jonas Mekas*: Mekas, in Coplans, *Andy Warhol*, 151.

150 *He said, "[A] hundred years from now"*: Stein and Plimpton, *Edie*, 234.

150 *When Tavel was asked*: Wilcock, *Autobiography and Sex Life*, 189.

151 *She told Tavel*: Watson, *Factory Made*, 217.

151 *There's a tape of her*: Painter and Weisman, *Edie: Girl on Fire,* 61.

155 *The entourage*: Illustrated in McCabe and Dalton, *Year in the Life*, 126–28.

157 Afternoon *is like a chamber opera*: McCabe and Dalton, *Year in the Life*, 130.

162 *No one knew*: Bockris, *Warhol: The Biography*, 228.

163 *By July*: Stein and Plimpton, *Edie*, 269–73.

164 *The caption*: *Vogue* 146, no. 2 (August 1, 1965): 86–91.

164 *Patti Smith really responded*: Stein and Plimpton, *Edie*, 243.

167 *And here's how she explained it*: Stein and Plimpton, *Edie*, 243.

167 *She wrote*: Nora Ephron, "Woman in the News: Edie Sedgwick, Superstar," *New York Post*, September 5, 1964, 2:1.

168 *As he put it*: Warhol and Hackett, *POPism*, 50–51.

169 *Viva, one of the later superstars in the Factory*: Stein and Plimpton, *Edie*, 226.

170 *Gerard told Victor Bockris*: Bockris, *Warhol: The Biography*, 185.

170 *And Andy's longtime friend*: Wilcock, *Autobiography and Sex Life*, 62–63.

170 *Plus, of course*: Wilcock, *Autobiography and Sex Life*, 34–35.

171 *Here's how radical the effect was*: Mekas, in Coplans, *Andy Warhol*, 139.

172 *Ondine says he didn't actually meet him*: Smith, *Warhol's Art and Films*, 423.

172 *Still, there are those*: Stein and Plimpton, *Edie*, 217; Painter and Weisman, *Edie: Girl on Fire*, 72.

174 *The package arrives*: Andy Warhol, *a: a novel* (New York: Grove Press, 1968), 30; Callie Angell, in *From Stills to Motion & Back Again: Texts on Andy Warhol's "Screen Tests" & "Outer and Inner Space,"* Geralyn Huxley et al. (Vancouver: Presentation House Gallery, 2003), 15.

176 *"Oh, Bonjourno!"*: Warhol, *a: a novel*, 73.

177  *"People came to the door"*: Warhol, *a: a novel*, 74.

177  *Then when they're alone*: Warhol, *a: a novel*, 115.

178  *"Divinity star"*: Warhol, *a: a novel*, 121.

178  *"And spit"*: Warhol, *a: a novel*, 125–26.

179  *I know it's my failure*: Stephen Koch, *Stargazer: The Life, World and Films of Andy Warhol* (New York and London: Marion Boyars, 1991, reprinted 2002), 67.

179  *Gerard Malanga said much the same thing*: Bockris, *Warhol: The Biography*, 220.

180  *He told Gretchen Berg*: Gretchen Berg, interview, *Los Angeles Free Press*, March 17, 1967.

181  *Her image on the television monitor says*: Angell, *From Stills to Motion*, 27–28.

181  *To give you an idea*: Angell, *From Stills to Motion*, 14–15.

183  *People in Dylan's circle*: Warhol and Hackett, *POPism*, 156.

184  *He claimed that he told Edie about it*: Watson, *Factory Made*, 233.

184  *Whatever the reason*: Bockris, *Warhol: The Biography*, 231.

184  *Brigid Berlin's sister Richie says*: Stein and Plimpton, *Edie*, 273–74.

184  *First thing in the morning*: Stein and Plimpton, *Edie*, 274–75.

185  *He told Andy later*: Warhol and Hackett, *POPism*, 153.

186  *Mel tried to tell her*: Warhol and Hackett, *POPism*, 156.

186  *Andy said Edie*: Warhol and Hackett, *POPism*, 161.

188  *In Andy's words*: Warhol and Hackett, *POPism*, 158.

188  *So when they were all out there on Fire Island*: Watson, *Factory Made*, 234.

189  *Bockris, however*: Bockris, *Warhol: The Biography*, 231.

189  *In Steven Watson's words*: Watson, *Factory Made*, 244.

190  *So on October 4*: Watson, *Factory Made*, 244–46.

192  *"When we walked"*: Warhol and Hackett, *POPism*, 166–67.

## NOTES FOR MY DEAD BROTHER

199  *But Chuck Wein*: Painter and Weisman, *Edie: Girl on Fire*, 91.

200  *Edie didn't understand*: Stein and Plimpton, *Edie*, 255.

200  *Patti Smith said it*: Stein and Plimpton, *Edie*, 243.

200  *But as Andy said*: Warhol, *The Philosophy*, 85.

201  *Patti Smith's description*: Stein and Plimpton, *Edie*, 254.

201  *But what Patti Smith saw*: Stein and Plimpton, *Edie*, 254.

202  *Now, however, celebrity means a person enjoying*: Wikipedia.

205  *But Andy did*: Warhol, *The Philosophy*, 144.

205  *As Gretchen Berg put it*: Wilcock, *Autobiography and Sex Life*, 31.

206  *"Sometimes people"*: Warhol, *The Philosophy*, 112.

207  *That time when he was being*: Shore and Tillman, *The Velvet Years*, 137.

208  *As Billy Name*: Shore and Tillman, *The Velvet Years*, 31.

209  *Here's what Steven Watson says of it*: Watson, *Factory Made*, 159–60.

209  *He was unfazed*: Watson, *Factory Made*, 174.

210  *He said, "Nowadays if you're a crook"*: Warhol, *The Philosophy*, 85.

211  *Edie was crying*: Watson, *Factory Made*, 265.

214  *His sense of existence*: Warhol, *The Philosophy*, 7.

214  *As Charles Henri Ford put it*: Wilcock, *Autobiography and Sex Life*, 57.

216  *There's also Gretchen Berg*: Wilcock, *Autobiography and Sex Life*, 30–31, 35.

216  *Then there's Ondine*: Smith, *Warhol's Art and Films*, 423.

217  *He said what he learned from Andy*: Wilcock, *Autobiography and Sex Life*, 180, 184.

217  *Andy himself said*: Warhol, *The Philosophy*, 33, 35.

218  *Sometime in the seventies*: Nora Ephron, *Scribble Scribble: Notes on the Media* (New York: Knopf, 1978), 155–56.

220  *Around that same time*: Gene Swenson, "What Is Pop Art? Answers from 8 Painters, Part 1," in *On & By Andy Warhol*, ed. G. Williams (London: Whitechapel Gallery; Cambridge, MA: MIT Press, 2016), 29.

222  *Apparently, the reason Andy painted all those* Deaths and Disasters: Wilcock, *Autobiography and Sex Life*, 67.

225  *As he put it, "I've always had a conflict"*: Warhol, *The Philosophy*, 147.

227  *He was fifteen when his father*: Stein and Plimpton, *Edie*, 410–12.

229  *Lance said*: Stein and Plimpton, *Edie*, 414.

230  *As his biographer*: Quoted by Michael Kruse, "Donald Trump Confronts a New Label: Loser," *Politico*, November 7, 2020.

232  *Sterling Morrison described* Shore and Tillman, *The Velvet Years*, 54.

233  *And like Andy himself*: Warhol, *The Philosophy*, 34–35.

240  *"Oh, Bonjourno!"*: Warhol, *a: a novel*, 73.

## ACKNOWLEDGMENTS

The inception of my project owes everything to the late Jean Stein, because without her I would never have brought myself to think about Edie in the first place or to face what happened; and the project itself owes everything to the following close friends to whom, one at a time over a period of years, I rather diffidently confided what I was up to: Deanne Urmy, with whom I discussed my idea and its form before I even began to write and at every stage thereafter; Miguel Tamen, who kindly read every version along the way, including all the false starts, and urged me on; Johanna Halford-MacLeod, whom I invited to be my research assistant and collaborator and who provided key insights and avenues to pursue, although in the end, owing to the pandemic, she wound up doing all the tedious work and having none of the fun; Peter Conrad, who understood everything and gave me all manner of essential advice; and lastly Jane Kramer and Vincent Crapanzano, who turned out to have known Warhol and various figures in the Factory in 1965, so their opinions were invaluable and their enthusiasm gave me confidence. I am especially grateful to my brother Jonathan for confirming dates and clarifying crucial facts despite his reluctance to have our story told yet again in public. To all of them, my heartfelt thanks.

But a project is not a book, and the book owes everything to Jonathan Galassi, who took my disorderly text and with the lightest of touches showed me how it might be shaped and focused. My gratitude to him is beyond measure. I am extremely grateful to Alex Merto, as well, for the stunning cover, and to the editorial assistant Katie Liptak for all her prompt and generous help, for her patience in responding to every question and accepting every inconvenient afterthought, and for her indulgence in allowing corrections on paper. In addition I should like to express my appreciation to Janet Rosenberg, the copy editor; to Janet Renard and Rima Weinberg, the proofreaders; to Janine Barlow, the production editor; and above all to Gretchen Achilles, the designer. I thank them all for the excellence of their work.

Finally, I owe particular debts of gratitude to Greg Pierce of the Warhol Museum and the Archives Study Center for his kindness in showing Johanna and me a number of the films that Warhol made with Edie; to Stephen Shore for talking to me about his experience in the Factory and for his generosity regarding permissions; to Steve Watson for sharing his wisdom and for all kinds of generous support; to Bob Bentley for his account of Katia's activities; to Kate Kohler Amory for her story and the image of Edie that she painted on her bedroom wall; to Johanna again for dealing with all the permissions and other business; to Ralph Lieberman for my picture on the jacket and for the pains he took preparing the illustrations; to Fronia W. Simpson for her invaluable help readying the text for submission; and to Karen Bucky and the staff of the library of the Clark Art Institute for all the hospitality and privileges accorded me during the many months I spent doing research.

# PERMISSIONS
# ACKNOWLEDGMENTS

Grateful acknowledgment is made for permission to reprint the following material:

Excerpts from Callie Angell, "Andy Warhol: *Outer and Inner Space*," in *From Stills to Motion and Back Again: Texts on Andy Warhol's "Screen Tests" & "Outer and Inner Space,"* ed. Geralyn Huxley et al. (Vancouver: Presentation House Gallery, 2003). Used by permission of the author and the Polygon Gallery.

Excerpts from *Edie: An American Biography.* Copyright © 1982 by Jean Stein. Reprinted by the permission of Russell & Volkening as agents for The Estate of George Plimpton, copyright © 1982 by George Plimpton.

Dialogue excerpts from Geralyn Huxley and Greg Pierce, *Andy Warhol's* The Chelsea Girls. Andy Warhol, *The Chelsea Girls* (1966), 16 mm film, black and white and color, sound, 204 minutes in double screen. © The Andy Warhol Museum, Pittsburgh, PA, a museum of Carnegie Institute. All rights reserved.

Excerpts from Melissa Painter and David Weisman, *Edie: Girl on Fire* (San Francisco: Chronicle Books, 2006). *Edie: Girl on Fire* ©

David Weisman. Used with permission of Chronicle Books LLC, San Francisco.

Excerpts from Steven Watson, *Factory Made: Warhol and the Sixties* (New York: Pantheon, 2003).

Excerpts from Victor Bockris, *Warhol: The Biography* (New York: Da Capo Press, 2003).

Excerpts from Stephen Shore and Lynne Tillman, *The Velvet Years: Warhol's Factory, 1965–67* (New York: Thunder's Mouth, 1995).

Excerpts from Stephen Koch, *Stargazer: The Life, World and Films of Andy Warhol* (New York and London: Marion Boyars, 1991, reprinted 2002).

# ILLUSTRATION CREDITS

21982320509932